4-95

CW01045460

AN ANGRY GOD?

AN ANGRY GOD?
THE BIBLICAL DOCTRINE OF WRATH, FINAL JUDGMENT AND HELL

Eryl Davies

EVANGELICAL PRESS OF WALES

Cover design by Digby Williams
Cover photograph courtesy of the Wales Tourist Board

Chapters 5-8 and 11 of this book were first published by the Evangelical Press of Wales in 1984 under the title *The Wrath of God.*

Published by the Evangelical Press of Wales
Bryntirion, Bridgend, Mid Glamorgan, CF31 4DX, Wales
Printed in Wales by WBC Print Ltd, Bridgend

CONTENTS

PREFACE

Chapters 5-8 and 11 of this book formed the substance of addresses delivered at the annual Ministers' Conference of the Evangelical Movement of Wales at Bala in June 1981. These chapters were then published by the Evangelical Press of Wales in 1984 under the title *The Wrath of God*.

I have since spoken and written frequently on the subject and I am grateful for permission to use part of my articles in *Evangelical Times* (January 1986, Oct./Nov. 1988) in Chapters 1 and 10. Chapters 3 and 4 are based on a British Evangelical Council paper I prepared for their Study Conference at High Leigh in March 1989.

In addition, I valued opportunities of discussing my material in Ministers' Fellowships and Conferences as well as with my own students in class at the Evangelical Theological College of Wales. On all these occasions I have been stimulated and challenged to continue my study of this crucial doctrine.

Mrs Elizabeth Pritchard, Menai Bridge, typed my original manuscript for *The Wrath of God*, and Mrs Sylvia Hills, Cardiff, typed the six additional chapters; the Indexes were prepared by Mrs Chris Connor of Cardiff. I am indebted to these three ladies for their assistance.

Although I take issue in this book with the arguments of several evangelicals and other scholars, yet I assure them that my only desire has been to elucidate and uphold biblical truth rather than indulge in vitriolics. The unity of the Lord's people is precious to me.

May God bless His truth in these pages, and stir us all in the faithful discharge of our responsibilities in these confused but challenging days of opportunity.

1
1974: A Contemporary Watershed

It is no longer fashionable to believe in or preach the ever-lasting punishment of unbelievers in hell. You may not be surprised, for modernist preachers have criticized the orthodox, biblical doctrine of hell for decades. Sadly and tragically, this is true and the point will be illustrated extensively in this section when the historical background to the present debate is outlined.

However, we are not referring to modernists in this opening chapter but rather to evangelicals. While there are some people who smile derisively if hell is even mentioned, growing numbers of evangelicals reject the doctrine of everlasting punishment in favour either of ultimate restoration or annihilation. There are varied adaptations of both universalism and annihilation but we shall focus our attention here on the growing popularity of the theory of annihilation. Some advocates of annihilation insist that unbelievers are destroyed at death. The more popular version among evangelicals, however, is that unbelievers are raised at the general resurrection but between the resurrection and the second death they suffer the just punishment of their sins. This is only for a limited period before they are annihilated under the righteous judgment of God. On this view, therefore, eternal punishment is only eternal in its effects, not in its pains and duration.

What is disturbing is that although a number of evangelical authors and publishers have recently expressed sympathy and, in some cases, support for annihilation, hardly a voice has been raised in protest. It will be helpful to refer to some of the more important publications which have contributed to the growing popularity of annihilation.

1974

The year 1974 is a watershed in the contemporary history of the doctrine of eternal punishment. Since 1974 the theory of annihilation has been made respectable in several areas of evangelicalism, particularly in Britain and the United States; this has been largely due to the wide and favourable publicity given to it in books and magazines as well as a more open attitude towards the theory.

In 1974 IVP published J.W. Wenham's *The Goodness of God* which was republished in 1985 under the new title, *The Enigma of Evil*. What is special about this book? After all, it is informative and stimulating, aiming to clarify practical difficulties over God's goodness in relation to providence and salvation. Furthermore, only one chapter (fifteen pages in fact) is actually devoted to the subject of hell, so why should this book be regarded as a watershed in the contemporary history of the doctrine?

Tentative

First of all, *The Goodness of God* was the first popular book by an evangelical author and publisher in which doubts about eternal punishment were expressed so forcefully and in which conditional immortality was tentatively put forward as a possible and more satisfactory alternative to eternal punishment. A new climate of opinion now prevails among evangelicals and this is immediately apparent when one compares the period 1974-1990 with the war and post-war years, for example, 1940-1965. Two examples can be given to illustrate this point.

An Anglican churchman, Harry E. Guillebaud (author of a helpful book, *Why The Cross?* first published in 1937, which assumed the doctrine of everlasting punishment) changed to an annihilationist position by 1940. While preparing his book *Some Moral Difficulties of the Bible* for the Inter-Varsity Fellowship he decided against including a chapter on eternal punishment. His reason was that he felt the need to research the subject in greater depth. As a result of further study, he wrote *The Righteous Judge* in which he strongly advocated conditional immortality/annihilation. Guillebaud returned for the last time to Africa in 1940 as Archdeacon of Ruanda-Urundi but died in 1941. Interestingly, no publisher was prepared to publish his manuscript and it was not until 1965 that the manuscript was eventually published but privately by the Rev. Bernard L. Bateson at the request of the author's widow.

Similarly, in the immediate post-war years, Dr Basil Atkinson, an Under Librarian in Cambridge University Library from 1925 to 1960, wrote in support of conditionalist views in his *Life and Immortality* which again had to be published privately. John Wenham acknowledges that 'suspicion of heresy has made it difficult for conditionalists to find reputable publishers, which has resulted in their views remaining unduly suspect'.[1] The situation has certainly changed. 1974, therefore, was a significant year for Christian publishing; a prominent and influential evangelical publishing house like IVP, which 'in earlier years would not touch Guillebaud or Basil Atkinson',[2] published Wenham's book in which the orthodox doctrine of eternal punishment is undermined and questioned.

Milestone

A second reason why Wenham's book can be regarded as a watershed in the contemporary history of the doctrine of hell is the way it has been acclaimed by conditionalists/annihilationists themselves as a milestone not only

1. John Wenham, *The Goodness of God* (Inter-Varsity Press, 1974), p.40. This is a useful but disturbing book.
2. Dr Robert E. D. Clark quoted in *Resurrection*, Oct.-Dec. 1986, p.14.

in Christian publishing but also in commending the theory of conditional immortality to a wider Christian public. At this point, we confine our examples to the Resurrection Fellowship which was formerly known as the Conditional Immortality Fellowship. This Fellowship is 'a movement within the Evangelical Christian community with members in a number of denominations who believe that immortality is in Christ alone. Man, not being immortal by nature is offered immortality as a gift which can only be received by faith in Jesus Christ as Lord and Saviour.'[3]

The Resurrection Fellowship has certainly made capital out of the publication in 1974 of Wenham's book. For example, in an introductory letter to librarians commending their new Study Guide, Bernard Bateson writes:

> A growing number are coming to the belief that man is not naturally immortal, and that the ultimate fate of the wicked will be utter and complete destruction. They are following in the footsteps of the late scholars, Archdeacon H.E. Guillebaud of Ruanda, Dr Basil F.C. Atkinson of Cambridge, and the Rev. J. Stafford Wright, Principal of Tyndale Hall, Bristol; and they are known as Conditionalists. Among these modern evangelical Christians we must mention the Rev. John W. Wenham, a former Vice-Principal of Tyndale Hall, whose book, *The Goodness of God*, appeared in 1974, later re-published as *The Enigma of Evil* (Inter-Varsity Press).

Another example appears in the same Study Guide in a detailed A-4 sized booklet entitled *What Others Have Said*. The aim of the booklet is to quote well-known scholars and church leaders who have espoused conditionalism. Quoting both liberal and evangelical scholars and leaders like Emil Brunner, Oscar Cullmann, Alan Richardson, John Stott, Norman Anderson and others, the final reference is to John W. Wenham with two quotations from *The Good-*

3. *Resurrection*, Special Issue, 1984, p.2.

ness of God. A further reference to Wenham's book is made by Dr Robert Clark in 1978 to the Rev. Bernard Bateson, editor of the *Resurrection* magazine:

> I am in sympathy with your views . . . I really thought the battle was won and was quite surprised to hear that young people when converted agonize over the subject as I did. Even the staid Inter-Varsity Fellowship has published John Wenham's book [*The Goodness of God*].[4]

While Wenham's book disturbed a few Christians, it was seen nevertheless as a major encouragement by conditionalists and a means of giving respectability and publicity to their theory amongst evangelicals.

Open-ended

There is a further reason why this 1974 publication should be regarded as a watershed in theology. In summarizing the debate between eternal punishment and conditional immortality, the author leaves the reader with the impression that he at least sympathizes with, if not favours, conditional immortality. This is despite his valuable warnings to those tempted to abandon the orthodox position. Note, for example, Wenham's conclusion:

> We shall consider ourselves under no obligation to defend the notion of unending torment until the arguments of the conditionalists have been refuted.[5]

This open-ended approach by Wenham, who has authored some valuable books, has misled and confused numbers of people and his brief chapter on hell has given greater respectability to the theory of annihilation – and this for the first time by an important evangelical publisher. Incidentally, it is interesting that most of the English advocates of conditional immortality have been evangelical

4. *Resurrection*, Oct.-Dec. 1986, p.14.
5. Wenham, *The Goodness of God*, p.41.

Anglicans although by today Christians from other denominations are being increasingly won over to the theory.

Signal

Finally, one important result of Wenham's chapter on hell in *The Goodness of God* was to encourage the advocates of conditional immortality to express themselves more publicly and boldly in support of their theory. The result is that since 1974 we have witnessed some significant articles in Christian magazines and theological journals, as well as books, all advocating conditional immortality. Was Wenham a signal to others to come into the open and declare their preference and support for annihilation? The publication of Wenham's book in 1974 by IVP represents a watershed in the contemporary history of the doctrine of eternal punishment. The republication of the book under a new title will serve only to undermine further the orthodox doctrine.

It was a year later in 1975 that the Rev. John Stott expressed his agnosticism concerning eternal punishment in an interview with the editor of *The Evangelical Magazine of Wales*. Affirming his belief in the reality and eternity of hell, Stott confessed he was prepared to remain agnostic as to whether unbelievers will be annihilated or not. 'Those who emphasize the time factor, who emphasize that hell will go on and on', he claimed, 'have not faced up to the problem of time'. Admittedly, it is difficult for us, bounded as we are by space and time, to conceive of eternity as being timeless. However, it is one thing to acknowledge this difficulty but quite a different matter to introduce as Stott does the possibility of annihilation or even universalism for unbelievers after hell. In the same year, John Stott reaffirmed 'a certain reverent and humble agnosticism about the precise nature of hell . . . but clear and definite we must be that hell is an awful, eternal reality'.[6]

6. *Christian Mission in the Modern World* (Falcon, 1975; republished in 1986 by Kingsway Publications), p.112.

In 1976, Hodder and Stoughton published *Issues of Life and Death,* authored by Sir Norman Anderson who is a former chairman of the House of Laity in the Church of England General Synod. Writing cautiously but firmly, the author believes it is equally valid to view condemnation 'in terms of a death and destruction which is "eternal" in the sense that it is final and irreversible'.[7]

Professor Howard Marshall's *Pocket Guide to Christian Beliefs* published by IVP in 1978 includes a brief reference to the debate concerning the nature of eternal punishment. The author tries to remove a number of misunderstandings which some have concerning the theory of annihilation.[8]

Alarming

An alarming and surprising statement of support for conditional immortality was published in 1979 by the Presbyterian and Reformed Publishing Company in the United States. This was *The Sovereignty of Grace* by Arthur C. Custance, a Reformed theologian in America. The book has disturbed some British readers because of its final section in Part Five entitled, 'The Future of the Non-elect'. The rest of the book is a helpful, lucid expression of the Five Points of Calvinism and contains a great deal of practical application. Perhaps this makes the book even more damaging in its influence. Notice, too, that this book represents another first by a reputable, orthodox publishing house, in which the idea of annihilation is circulated approvingly among evangelicals and as part of a larger work.

Custance's book marks a significant shift in policy on the part of the publishers in relation to the doctrine of eternal punishment. For example, in 1957 they published Harry Buiss's *The Doctrine of Eternal Punishment,* which

7. Sir Norman Anderson, *Issues of Life and Death* (Hodder & Stoughton, 1976), p.29.
8. Howard Marshall, *Pocket Guide to Christian Beliefs* (Inter-Varsity Press, 1978), p.136.

the late Professor John Murray described as 'a candid forthright witness to the reality of hell',[9] and in which Buiss argues convincingly against annihilation. Within 22 years of the publication of Buiss's book, the same publisher issued Custance's book with its strong bias against eternal punishment.

On Custance's own admission, his thinking is biased; he speaks, for example, of 'the bias I have . . . which tends towards a somewhat more helpful view than is current today in some segments of the evangelical community',[10] and he was greatly influenced by the conditionalist writings of Andrew Jukes, A. Farrer, A.T. Hanson and Samuel Cox. His approach is also dangerously speculative[11] and rationalistic. Criticising the belief that hell is as eternal as heaven (remember that the same Greek word *aiōnios*, 'everlasting', in Matthew 25:46 is used of heaven and hell), Custance claims that 'one cannot rationally introduce the idea of a harsher or milder punishment if both are interminable . . .'[12] But why not, for our Lord spoke of degrees of punishment (e.g. Matthew 11:22-24; Luke 12:47-48)? Not only does Custance rationalize his way through this section, he also minimizes the gravity and awfulness of sin against God. His phrase, 'temporal offence', is particularly misleading and betrays a superficial and inadequate view of sin committed against God.

Another significant book was published by Hodder and Stoughton in 1982, written by Stephen Travis under the title, *I Believe in the Second Coming of Jesus*. Once again this is a generally helpful and popular book, read widely by young people, yet it seriously undermines the doctrine of

9. *Collected Writings of John Murray* (Banner of Truth, 1982), vol.4, p.305.
10. Arthur C. Custance, *The Sovereignty of Grace* (Presbyterian and Reformed Publishing Company, 1979), p.315.
11. ibid., p.313.
12. ibid., p.320.

eternal punishment. 'If pressed', remarks Travis, 'I must myself opt for annihilationism . . .'[13]

Also in 1982, Verdict Publications published E.W. Fudge's *The Fire that Consumes.* An American evangelical, Fudge argues strongly for conditional immortality. 'Does the Word of God teach the eternal conscious torment of the lost?' asks Fudge. 'Our modest study', he replies, 'fails to show that it does.' Uncompromisingly, he claims that

> traditionalist authors have never . . . taken up the numerous passages in support of final extinction, to show where conditionalists have either misused the text, ignored the context, eliminated crucial information, or added data not found in the Word of God itself.[14]

This is an exaggerated claim for in the history of the doctrine of eternal punishment there have been some lucid and convincing presentations of the orthodox position which have also included an exposure of annihilationism. We must acknowledge, however, that very little has been written in the last three or four decades clarifying and upholding the orthodox doctrine and at the same time interacting with the flood of conditionalist/annihilationist writings in recent years. This book, however, aims to do this and to face the challenge of conditionalism. Incidentally, Edward Fudge published an article in 1984 in the *Journal of the Evangelical Theological Society* in America in which he favoured 'irreversible extinction'. The article is simplistic in places and disappointing in terms of competent exegesis and thoroughness, but the message is loud and clear; he favours annihilation. By contrast, Vernon

---

13. Stephen Travis, *I Believe in the Second Coming of Jesus* (Hodder & Stoughton, 1982), p.198.
14. E.W. Fudge, *The Fire That Consumes* (Verdict Publications, 1982), p.434.

Grounds wrote a more able and stimulating article in the same journal strongly supporting the orthodox position.[15]

Perhaps the most devastating book to appear in undermining the doctrine of the unending conscious punishment of unbelievers in hell is *Essentials.* Published early in 1988 by Hodder and Stoughton, it is cast in dialogue form between the liberal scholar, David Edwards, and the evangelical, John Stott. This is both a disturbing and helpful book. It is disturbing because of Edwards's strongly liberal approach to major biblical doctrines, yet much of what John Stott writes by way of reply is helpful.

However, the book is disturbing for another reason. Despite having produced so many books over the past thirty years, this is the first book in which Stott expresses in print his views on hell. Edwards draws attention to Stott's past silence[16] which Stott himself acknowledges and explains over several pages. Stott finds the concept of everlasting, conscious punishment 'intolerable'[17] although he has 'a great respect' for the doctrine and does 'not lightly set it aside, and partly because the unity of the worldwide Evangelical constituency has always meant much to me'. He thinks that Scripture points in the direction of annihilation. This is a position he holds 'tentatively'; while he refuses to 'dogmatise'[18] about it, Stott is much more dogmatic in his view than he suggests. The issue is expressed by Stott in the following way: 'will the final destiny of the impenitent be eternal conscious torment . . . or will it be a total annihilation of their being?' Is everlasting punishment only 'a tradition which has to yield to the supreme authority of Scripture?'[19] Stott then offers four arguments in favour of annihilation and these will be considered later

15. *Journal of the Evangelical Theological Society,* September 1981.
16. David Edwards and John Stott, *Essentials* (Hodder & Stoughton, 1988), p.292.
17. ibid., p.314.
18. ibid., p.320.
19. ibid., pp.314-15.

in the book. The respected position of John Stott means that his views on annihilation will be accepted by many evangelicals worldwide without careful consideration of the orthodox position.

Another evangelical who has written recently in support of conditional immortality is Philip Edgcumbe Hughes. His book, *The True Image – The Origin and Destiny of Man in Christ*, was published by Inter-Varsity Press in 1989. The main thrust of the book is that

> not only the destiny but also the origin of man involves a profound relationship with the Second Person of the Holy Trinity. Indeed, mankind's destiny in Christ is precisely the fruition of mankind's origin in Christ.[20]

Within this context, Philip Hughes argues for, and defends, conditional immortality.

> The everlasting existence side by side . . . of heaven and hell would seem to be incompatible with the purpose and effect of the redemption achieved by Christ's coming. Sin with its consequences of suffering and death is foreign to the design of God's creation. The renewal of creation demands the elimination of sin and suffering and death.[21]

Paul Helm has reviewed this book helpfully and refers to 'the basic theological flaw' and 'other serious ones' in this book.[22]

One could refer to other books/articles recently published in which evangelicals advocate or sympathize with annihilationism but the foregoing details illustrate the claim that Wenham's *The Goodness of God* represents a watershed in the history of this doctrine. His book encouraged advocates of conditional immortality to express and argue their views more publicly.

20. Philip Edgcumbe Hughes, *The True Image – The Origin and Destiny of Man in Christ* (Inter-Varsity Press, 1989), p.viii.
21. ibid., p.405.
22. *Banner of Truth*, March 1990, p.28.

Thankfully, there has been a small number of articles/ books published during the eighties by evangelicals in which the orthodox doctrine of everlasting punishment has been upheld and argued for most convincingly.

A most useful book was published in 1982 by the Overseas Missionary Fellowship and authored by Dr Dick Dowsett entitled *God, That's Not Fair*. The sub-title is: *Letters to a young Christian challenging him to accept the Bible's teaching about Hell and judgment, and to do something about it.* In his preface, the author observes 'there has been a widespread running away from the fact of Hell and what it means, even in evangelical circles'.[23] In a helpful, penetrating way, Dick Dowsett urges believers to take seriously the biblical teaching on hell and, at the same time, to warn people of this awful danger.

In 1984, my own book, *The Wrath of God*, was first published by the Evangelical Press of Wales. The contents of this book formed the substance of addresses delivered at a Ministers' Conference in 1981 aimed at elucidating the biblical doctrine of wrath, final judgment and hell yet in a strongly pastoral, contemporary context. The present book is a major revision and expansion of the earlier 1984 edition. A useful, evangelistic book was published by Evangelical Press in 1985 under the title, *How Can a God of Love Send People to Hell?* The author was John Benton. This book is a concise and readable introduction to the scriptural teaching on hell.

For the *Evangelical Times* in January 1986 I wrote a feature article on 'Everlasting Punishment' in which I alerted believers to the growing popularity of annihilationism. What surprised me was the number of letters I received from ET readers favouring annihilation. I assume that the silent majority of readers agreed with me, but did they?

During 1986, the Banner of Truth republished W.G.T.

23. Dick Dowsett, *God, That's Not Fair* (Overseas Missionary Fellowship, 1982), p.ix.

Shedd's *The Doctrine of Endless Punishment* (first published in 1885). In the first section of the book, we are given a brief history of the doctrine while the second section provides a detailed consideration of the biblical data. Shedd rightly argues that 'the chief objections to the doctrine of Endless Punishment are not biblical but speculative'.[24]

In 1987 my own book, *Condemned For Ever!* with the sub-title, *What the Bible Teaches about Eternal Punishment*, was published by Evangelical Press. This book was intended as a simple, 'popular' presentation of the Bible's teaching on this sombre subject and a challenge to prevailing secular ideas.

Another important publication by Banner of Truth on this subject was *The Last Things*. This book was published in 1989 and the author, Paul Helm, deals helpfully with the subjects Death, Judgment, Heaven and Hell. The author's purpose is 'not to speculate, or to sentimentalize, but to state as sharply and starkly as possible the plain facts of the matter as Scripture portrays them.'[25] Paul Helm demonstrates clearly that 'the arguments for annihilation are weak, even interpreted charitably. But they appear immeasurably weaker when the positive teaching of Scripture about life after death is added.'[26]

In conclusion, I refer to a conference promoted by the National Association of Evangelicals in America and held in May 1989 at Trinity Evangelical Divinity School in Deerfield, Illinois. 350 Christian leaders convened for this four-day conference and among those who presented papers were Carl Henry, J.I. Packer, Don Carson, David Wells, Harold O.J. Brown and Kenneth Kantzer. There was disagreement in the conference concerning annihilationism.

24. W.G.T. Shedd, *The Doctrine of Endless Punishment* (Banner of Truth, 1986), p.118.
25. Paul Helm, *The Last Things* (Banner of Truth, 1989), p.13.
26. ibid., p.119.

Dr Packer informed the conference that John Stott had become a proponent of conditional immortality/annihilation. He then described conditionalism as a 'proposed revision of historical evangelical soteriology, the view that the question of salvation is less agonizing than we thought because after the judgment day the unsaved will not exist'.[27] Dr Packer went on to stress that this view robs evangelism of its urgency. *Reformation Today* reports that 'the conference was evenly divided on whether to include a clause which would renounce annihilationism. In the event a renunciation clause was omitted.'[28] The conference papers have been published by Zondervan under the title, *Evangelical Affirmations* and edited by Kenneth S. Kantzer and Carl F.H. Henry.

Having now illustrated the growing popularity of annihilation/conditional immortality among evangelicals, we will proceed in the next chapter to outline the historical background to this debate before finally pinpointing some contemporary objections to the biblical doctrine of hell.

27. Kenneth S. Kantzer and Carl F.H. Henry (eds.), *Evangelical Affirmations* (Zondervan, 1989), pp.123-4.
28. *Reformation Today*, vol. 110, July/August 1989, p.32

2
The Decline of Hell
Historical and Contemporary Perspective

As early as the seventeenth century, members of different church denominations questioned and denied the doctrine of eternal punishment.[1] John Locke, the famous English philosopher, was only one of many religious intellectuals who rejected the orthodox doctrine of hell; like Isaac Newton, Samuel Clark and William Whiston, Locke was an Arian in his beliefs. Thomas Hobbes, especially by his theory that punishment should be reformatory in purpose, had helped further to undermine the orthodox doctrine. The Puritan theologian, John Owen, answered many of their arguments competently, particularly those which Peter Sterry and Jeremiah White used.[2] While some sixteenth century English Anabaptists and seventeenth century Socinians advocated annihilation, Locke and Whiston believed that the wicked would be annihilated only after suffering an appropriate period of torment in hell; this is the position currently favoured by many conditionalists today, including John Stott.

The rise of biblical criticism, Darwin's evolutionary theory of the world's origins and Bentham's view of punishment all contributed in the nineteenth century to a further undermining of the biblical teaching on hell. By the end of the nineteenth century, W.E. Gladstone expressed his alarm that the doctrine of hell was no longer preached:

1. For details, see D.P. Walker, *The Doctrine of Hell: Seventeenth-Century Discussion of Eternal Torment* (Routledge & Kegan Paul, 1964).
2. See Owen's 'Diatriba de Justitia Divina' in vol.10 of his *Works* (Banner of Truth, 1966).

A portion of Divine truth, which even if secondary is so needful, appears to be silently passing out of view, and ... the danger of losing it ought at all costs to be averted ...[3]

The situation, of course, was not quite as bleak as Gladstone had claimed for there was a minority of ministers who continued to preach eternal punishment. Nevertheless, influential Protestant denominations both in Europe and America had by this time rejected hell as an unacceptable and offensive doctrine. Geoffrey Rowell describes accurately the general nineteenth-century situation regarding the eternal punishment of the wicked:

... men felt that old certainties were being eroded by new knowledge, and in which an optimistic faith in progress co-existed uneasily with forebodings of the consequences of increasingly rapid social change. A Bible whose Divine authority had been accepted rather than argued about was battered by blasts of German criticism and scientific theory ... God ... was increasingly repudiated as an immoral tyrant; and the hell to which the wicked were consigned ... became a stumbling-block to believers and a weapon of attack for secularists.[4]

From the 1840s onwards, the doctrine of eternal punishment was at the centre of the theological debate, particularly in England. Books, articles, tracts and sermons were published on the subject and there were attempts to discipline those who questioned the orthodox doctrine. During the 1870s, immortality and the future life became the dominant issue with a more tolerant attitude shown

3. W.E. Gladstone, *Studies subsidiary to the Works of Bishop Butler* (1896), pp.199,121.
4. Geoffrey Rowell, *Hell and the Victorians: A Study of the Nineteenth-Century Theological Controversies concerning Eternal Punishment and the Future Life* (Oxford: Clarendon Press, 1974), p.vii.

towards the theory of conditional immortality. By the eighties and nineties, the shift was rather marked in the direction of social concern and politics. Briefly, we can retrace our steps by referring to some of the more well-known characters and incidents in the debate on eternal punishment earlier in the nineteenth century.

Frederick Denison Maurice was dismissed in 1853 from his professorial chair at King's College, London because he criticized the doctrine of eternal punishment. Although many thought that he was a universalist, Maurice denied it. However, there were several significant influences which all contributed to Maurice's denial of eternal punishment.

First of all, there was his father's Unitarian beliefs and, secondly, Irving's claim that the incarnation of Jesus Christ was supremely the self-manifestation of God to man rather than a means to the Atonement. A third influence on Maurice was S.T. Coleridge who regarded hell as 'morally intolerable'; his theology was a mixture of mysticism and Unitarianism. Thomas Erskine of Linlathen was another influence on Maurice's theology. His *True and False Religion* published in 1820 taught that all people are already forgiven by God. It was in 1833 and in London that Erskine first met Maurice; both agreed that the Greek *aiōnios* refers to man's spiritual state, not endless duration. Erskine believed that '. . . eternal death is living in self'.

As early as 1844, Maurice taught that God's purpose in creating the world was not the distribution of rewards and punishments but the knowledge of Himself which includes eternal life. According to Maurice, the wicked continued to be 'alienated from goodness and truth' and such a state was 'to be in the deepest pit of hell'. But it was the *Theological Essays* in 1853 which led to his dismissal from King's College. Here he repeated his qualitative view of both eternal life and death. 'What then is death eternal', he asks, 'but to be without God?' There was a mixed reception to his essays. The Unitarians welcomed them but the Wesleyan Methodists warned members to avoid 'this new, complex and deadly heresy, which is little better than a modern Gnosticism of a refined character'.[5]

A more famous incident was the lawsuit brought against the Rev. H.B. Wilson. He had already aroused suspicion for his Bampton Lectures in 1851 but his essay on the national church in the volume, *Essays and Reviews*, published in 1860, led to the introduction of legal proceedings against him. In his essay, Wilson asked for a greater comprehensiveness in the national church and preferred a man's moral qualities rather than doctrinal orthodoxy. He concluded his essay by encouraging Anglicans to:

> entertain a hope that there shall be found, after the great adjudication, receptacles suitable for those who shall be infants (that is, the wicked who do not attain to Christian perfection;) not as to years of terrestrial life, but as to spiritual development – nurseries as it were and seed-grounds, where the undeveloped may grow up under new conditions – the stunted may become strong and the perverted restored . . .[6]

In June 1862, Wilson was suspended from his living for one year but Wilson's appeal to the judicial committee of the Privy Council was upheld in February 1864.[7] Significantly, some eleven thousand Anglican clergymen, both Tractarians and Evangelicals, signed the *Oxford Declaration* (1864) against Wilson and the other essayists. They linked a confession of faith in the inspiration of Scripture with the doctrine of eternal punishment, insisting that the Church of England believed and taught 'in the words of our Blessed Lord, that "the punishment" of the "cursed" equally with the "life" of the "righteous" is "everlasting"'.

---

5. *London Quarterly Review*, 1854-5, pp.433,436.
6. *Essays and Reviews*, 1860, pp.205-26.
7. Fendable V. Wilson, *Ecclesiastical Cases relating to Doctrine* (1865), pp.247-90.

Writing in a *Pastoral Letter* in 1864, Archbishop Thomson of York maintained that 'everlasting must mean lasting for ever, never coming to an end' and warned that changing this meaning would disturb people's faith in the plain statements of the Bible.

The Evangelical Alliance was also involved in the debate on eternal punishment. In fact, the 1860 *Essays and Reviews* had helped to push the doctrine of Scripture and eternal punishment further into the arena of public debate. For the Evangelical Alliance, controversy surrounded its secretary, T.R. Birks. One of the leaders of evangelicals in England, Birks had written several books including *Difficulties of Belief in Connexion with Creation and the Fall* (1855), *Victory of Divine Goodness, The Ways of God* (1863) and *The Atonement* (1876). Already, the earlier books had indicated changes in Birks's theology as well as similarities with the theology of Maurice. According to Birks, the relationship of divine justice and mercy was the major question relating to eternal punishment. Birks viewed these two attributes only as a contrast, not an absolute contradiction. Accepting a universal atonement, he went on to suggest that divine justice did not exclude the lost from some passive but real contemplation of the divine goodness.

Two factors in particular helped to put pressure on Birks. Firstly, many evangelicals were convinced that eternal punishment was a crucially important doctrine; the rejection of this doctrine involved, sooner or later, the modification of other fundamental truths. Secondly, due to American concern over the growing popularity of universalist and annihilationist teachings, the Evangelical Alliance Confession of Faith had been expanded in 1846 to include a clause on eternal punishment. A significant number of members, therefore, felt that Birks's writings, especially his *Victory of Divine Goodness*, represented a denial of the Alliance's position on eternal punishment. Birks insisted that he still taught eternal punishment but

R. Baxter clearly showed that Birks had reinterpreted the doctrine substantially. Would Birks use the plain words of Scripture alone to put an end to the debate and speculation? It was a reasonable request but Birks resigned as Secretary of the Evangelical Alliance after nineteen years of service, but further attempts to expel him from membership of the Alliance failed. 'It is an indication of the changed climate', writes Geoffrey Rowell, 'that only sixteen members felt so strongly about the dispute that they resigned.'[8] Birks's continuing membership of the Alliance and his subsequent appointment as a Cambridge professor illustrates the growing tolerance by the late 1860s among evangelicals concerning the nature of eternal punishment.

Eternal hope

During November and December 1877, the then Archdeacon of Westminster, F.W. Farrer, preached a series of sermons on eternal punishment. The most controversial was 'Hell, what it is not' preached on 11 November. Not surprisingly, the sermons aroused considerable interest and they were published in 1878 under the title *Eternal Hope*. While rejecting eternal punishment, Farrer was unable to accept any of the alternatives such as conditionalism, purgatory or universalism.

Both universalists and conditionalists wrote books which were controversial and often divisive. One of the leading universalists in the 1870s was Andrew Jukes whose *The Second Death and the Restitution of All Things* (1867) was influential. However, because of his views he was forced to leave his independent Baptist Church in Hull a year later and he entered the Anglican ministry at Highgate. While serving as a Baptist pastor at Southsea in 1852, Samuel Cox also became a universalist. He gave a series of lectures in Nottingham in which he suggested the possibility of probation after death. These lectures were

8. Rowell, *Hell and the Victorians*, p.128.

published in 1877 under the title *Salvator Mundi*. There was no strong reaction to the book but in 1884 the publishers of the *Expositor* journal which Cox edited asked him to promise to exclude from the journal in future 'all allusions to "the larger hope"' but Cox was unable to make this promise and resigned as editor. His church at Southsea, however, remained supportive.

Conditionalism

It was among the Baptists and Congregationalists in England that conditionalism established a firm footing. Henry Hamlet Dabney (1809-1884), for example, was pastoring a Baptist church in Maidstone and he published in 1844 his *Notes of Lectures on Future Punishment*. While holding an orthodox view of eternal punishment, he preached a powerful sermon on the words of the Lord Jesus Christ, 'these shall go away into everlasting punishment' (Matthew 25:46). After the sermon, Dabney questioned the soundness of his own teaching and decided to research the subject in depth. He felt that the debate rested on the fact whether or not the soul is immortal. His conclusion was a negative one which he reached only after considerable mental anguish; 'I wallowed on the floor of my locked study in agony', he writes, 'lest I should, on the one hand, give up and oppose a mighty truth, or on the other, refuse clearer light.' Dabney was criticized in *The Evangelical Magazine* but the secretary of the British and Foreign Schools Society, Henry Dunn, defended Dabney and later authored a book in support of conditionalism.

A young Congregational minister in Hereford, Edward White, also published in 1844 a tract commending conditionalism; the title was *What is the Fall?* Born in 1819 in London, White reacted against the Calvinism of his pastor, George Clayton, at York Street Congregational Church in Walworth; Clayton was also one of the leading Congregational theologians of the period. The doctrines of election and reprobation, writes White,

> nearly drove me mad with secret misery of mind, in thinking of such a God . . . From fourteen years old and upwards our faith depended very much on the art of not thinking on the hateful mystery.'[9]

After spending two years in Glasgow University, White left in 1838 without a degree but was soon strongly influenced by James Fontaine's conditionalist work *Eternal Punishment* (1817). White feared that he would be excluded from Congregational pulpits on account of his conditionalist teaching but this did not materialize until 1851. It was White's *Life in Christ* published in 1845 which provoked many protests in dissenting churches and led to White's rejection by many fellowships.

One critic of White's conditionalism was the Baptist theologian, John Howard Hinton. His book, *Athanasia*, argued that conditionalists like White had not considered the evidence for and against man's natural immortality in a sufficiently detached and objective manner. Hinton agreed that man's immortality was a gift from God, not a necessary attribute of his nature, but he insisted that immortality was a gift bestowed on all people at their creation and not on a restricted number at conversion.[10]

What was popularly called the 'Life in Christ' controversy began in the columns of the *Christian World* with a discussion between Dr Angus, Andrew Jukes and Edward White. Here White insisted that the use of the term 'annihilation' in the debate was unhelpful and he preferred to talk of physical and spiritual death so as not to be identified with secular annihilationists. Despite White's appeal, the label 'annihilationist' was a common description of conditionalists at this time.

9. For further reading, see F.A. Freer, *Edward White, His Life and Work* (1902).
10. J.H. Hinton, *Theological Works* (1864), iii, 1,7,28,30.

Dr R.W. Dale, the famous Congregational preacher of Carr's Lane, Birmingham, was one of many prominent preachers and church leaders won over to conditionalism; Dale declared his acceptance of this theory in 1874.[11] Two years later, the first of a series of conditionalist conferences was held in London and reports of these conferences were widely circulated especially among missionaries and ministers. Various conditionalist subjects were handled in these conferences. For example, Constable dismissed the doctrine of immortality as an expression of human pride while William Leask indicated the relationship of conditionalism to missionary theology. Arthur Mursell illustrated how secularists used the orthodox doctrine of eternal punishment as a weapon to attack and ridicule Christianity. Henry Drummond[12] wrote on eternal life and argued that Christians were misguided to try and prove natural immortality on the basis of philosophy or physiology.

Twentieth Century

Perhaps one of the best introductions to the twentieth century as regards the attitude of church leaders in England to the doctrine of hell is the intriguing symposium *Is There a Hell?* published in 1913 and co-authored by 16 men.[13]

In the Introduction we are informed:

> Of recent years there has been more talk in the pulpit of heaven than of hell, and not a few people have endeavoured to persuade themselves that there is no hell.[14]

Later, the writer affirms: 'There is a hell; that is incontrovertible, because there is good and bad. Its actual character remains a mystery, but its existence is clear.'[15]

11. A.W.W. Dale, *Life of R.W. Dale* (1898).
12. Drummond was the editor of *Natural Law in the Spiritual World* (1890).
13. Published by Cassell and Company, London & New York.
14. ibid., p.2.
15. ibid., p.4.

The author of Chapter Two, Silas K. Hocking, attempts to answer the question, 'What is Hell Like?' His answer is predictable and he advances a cautious universalism. By far the most interesting part of this chapter is the first page or so where he gives us a clear historical perspective. Hocking begins by referring to the Wesleyan Catechism he learned as a child:

Q: What sort of a place is hell?

A: Hell is a dark and bottomless pit of fire and brimstone.

Q: How will the wicked be punished there?

A: The wicked will be punished in hell by having their bodies tormented by fire and their souls by a sense of the wrath of God.

Q: How long will these torments last?

A: The torments of hell will last for ever and ever.

This catechism was published early in the nineteenth century by the Wesleyan Book Room but these questions and answers had been deleted long before the end of that century. However, Hocking maintains that until about 1885 'The idea of a material hell of fire was very generally taught in the churches.'[16] He then traces 'the revolt' against the doctrine which was 'very largely assisted' by the novels of George Macdonald and, later, by Samuel Cox's *Salvator Mundi* and Farrer's *Eternal Hope* in which the pulpit teaching on hell was shown to be 'an unauthorised accretion to the true doctrine, and was unsupported by Scripture as well as being repugnant to reason'.

Other chapter headings indicated the general message of the book: 'A Material Hell Absurd', 'Graduated Punishment', 'No Eternal Condemnation', and 'Hell that is Manmade'. One of the most vehement critics of the orthodox doctrine in the book was the Rev. A.J. Waldron:

16. ibid., p.13.

> If the Bible teaches 'everlasting punishment', so much
> the worse for the Bible, because we cannot believe it;
> you may quote texts and have behind the texts the very
> finest scholarship to justify certain interpretations, but
> it is no good. We are no longer the slaves of a book, nor
> the blind devotees of a creed; we believe in love and in
> evolution.[17]

Later, Waldron describes eternal punishment as 'absolutely impossible; for God to punish a man for ever, without a chance of the punishment serving the purpose of reform, is diabolical; no person with a spark of human emotion could assent to such a creed'.[18]

Some writers like Dr F.B. Meyer, the Revs Dinsdale T. Young and A.C. Dixon argued strongly for the biblical doctrine of hell. The latter, in the closing chapter underlined the scriptural teaching and used three principles to show the rightness of the wicked being punished in hell. Firstly, it is right to separate the bad from the good; secondly, it is right to punish sin and, thirdly, it is right to have degrees of punishment.

However, a famous Baptist preacher, Dr W. Graham Scroggie, embraced the teaching of conditional immortality. He was trained at Spurgeon's College and held pastorates at Leytonstone (1889-1903), Halifax (until 1905), Charlotte Chapel in Edinburgh (from 1916) and Metropolitan Tabernacle in London from 1938 to 1944. Dr Scroggie also exercised an extensive Bible-teaching ministry in many countries and was a regular Keswick speaker. It was in 1948 that Dr Scroggie first met R.E. Le Froom, the Seventh Day Adventist author of *The Prophetic Faith of Our Fathers*. They corresponded regularly and Froom provided Scroggie with a number of leaflets and books which advocated conditionalism. In 1955, Dr Froom visited the elderly and sick Dr Scroggie in London and was greeted with the

17. ibid., p.31.
18. ibid., p.32.

words: 'Brother Froom, I believe that God has raised you up for this great task . . . You may quote me whenever and wherever you please as being a believer in Conditionalism.'[19]

Rejection

Despite valiant attempts to defend biblical truths, the almost universal rejection by churches of hell and other biblical doctrines became even more apparent as the twentieth century proceeded.

In 1936, for example, Professor D.M. Baillie could write confidently that hell is 'open to serious objection . . . it can hardly be held adequate to the truth of Christianity'.[20] Barth's universalism, Tillich's existentialism and William Barclay's liberalism further undermined the orthodox doctrine in churches and colleges. 'The doctrine of an absolutely opposite eternal destiny of individuals', wrote Paul Tillich, 'cannot be defended'.[21] By 1967, Peter Hamilton could claim that 'the church today seldom mentions hell'.[22] Writing in 1980, Hendrikus Berkhof (not to be confused with Louis Berkhof) is representative of contemporary theologians in his candid rejection of the orthodox doctrine of hell:

> The ease with which many orthodox Christians used to and still designate at least 95% of the human race as lost betrays much thoughtlessness and harshness. Fortunately, secularism and the intense contact with non-Christian worlds compel us to a deeper and more careful consideration of this matter.[23]

19. Quoted in *Resurrection*, Oct.-Dec. 1986, p.5.
20. D.M. Baillie, *And the Life Everlasting* (Oxford University Press, 1936), p.243.
21. Paul Tillich, *Systematic Theology* (London: James Nisbet, 1964), vol.3, p.434.
22. Peter Hamilton, *The Living God and the Modern World* (Hodder & Stoughton, 1967), p.135.
23. Hendrikus Berkhof, *Christian Faith* (Grand Rapids: Eerdmans, 1980), p.531.

Possibly the most popular condemnation of the doctrine of hell recently is by Robert Short (the author of *The Gospel According to Peanuts*) in a book published in 1983 with the title, *The Gospel from Outer Space*. Written against the background of the film ET and with the effective use of cartoons, the author devotes at least one chapter to denouncing the orthodox doctrine of hell, claiming that 'the threat of eternal damnation prevents a proper understanding of the goodness of "the good news" of Christ . . .'[24]

Objections

Such examples could be multiplied but it will be more useful to notice, briefly, some of the reasons given by people for rejecting the biblical doctrine. The major reasons can be classified in a fourfold way, namely – philosophical, theological, hermeneutical and ethical.

In addition to the total depravity of human nature blinding the mind and making it averse to God and His self-revelation, *philosophical* reasons and presuppositions are also basic in determining the theological and hermeneutical approach to the subject of hell. We confine ourselves briefly by way of illustration to two contemporary philosophers. The first is John Hick, a trained philosopher who is now the H.G. Wood Professor of Theology in the University of Birmingham. His books, especially *Evil and the God of Love*[25] and also *Death and Eternal Life*, include numerous arguments against the doctrine of eternal punishment. He writes, for example, of the 'evident incongruity, if not self-contradiction, in the very notion of perpetual torment'.[26] In an orderly manner he also marshals all the objections and arguments against the orthodox

---

24. Robert Short, *The Gospel from Outer Space*, Fount Paperbacks (Collins, 1983), p.73.
25. John Hick, *Evil and the God of Love*, Fount Paperbacks (Collins, 1979).
26. John Hick *Death and Eternal Life*, Fount Paperbacks (Collins, 1979), p.199.

position:

> for the conscious creature to undergo physical and mental torture through unending time (if this is indeed conceivable) is horrible and disturbing beyond words; and the thought of such torment being deliberately inflicted by divine decree is totally incompatible with the idea of God as infinite love; the absolute contrast of heaven and hell, entered immediately after death, does not correspond to the innumerable gradations of human good and evil; justice could never demand for finite human sins the infinite penalty of eternal pain; such unending torment could never serve any positive or reformative purpose precisely because it never ends; and it renders any coherent Christian theodicy impossible by giving the evils of sin and suffering an eternal lodgment within God's creation.[27]

A second example is Brian Hebblethwaite who argues 'metaphysically . . . that the final state of created being will be good without qualification, and the existence of hell would undoubtedly introduce a major permanent qualification'. Hebblethwaite then concludes that 'religious agnosticism about God's eternal plans for the created universe is an inevitable stance for the reflective theist'.[28] These writers do not make any appeal to the Bible as their supreme authority but rather human reasoning is the criterion for deciding what is 'true' or acceptable.

The theological objection centres around the alleged incompatibility of the divine wrath and love. 'Guided by the universal scope of divine love,' remarks Peter C. Hodgson, 'Christian hope will rebel against every doctrinal restriction which sets limits to the vision of hope'.[29] Another theologian suggests that the reason why the church today

27. ibid., pp.200-1.
28. Brian Hebblethwaite, *Evil, Suffering and Religion* (London: Sheldon Press, 1976), pp.102-4.
29. Peter C. Hodgson, *Christian Theology: An Introduction to its Traditions and Tasks* (SPCK, 1983), p.296.

seldom mentions hell is 'because we have at last learned the truth that God is love and that the divine love predominates over the divine justice. I do not myself see how one can possibly combine God's love with the idea of eternal punishment . . .' Critics refuse to accept the harmony of the biblical approach that the divine love is also a holy, righteous love exercised consistently by God. Modern theology has created its own perverted image of God.

Hermeneutically, the doctrine of eternal punishment is more often dismissed as mythological and figurative or symbolic. The late John Robinson, for example, wrote: '. . . life can be hell . . . for that is really what hell is about – the dark side, the shadow side, of life . . .' He then describes three kinds of experiences which he described as 'hell':

> 1. Experiences of suffering, frightfulness and torture – physical or mental . . . 2. Experiences of madness – when reality, or the loss of reality, becomes unendurable. Many representations of hell have in fact been psychotic – descriptions of a nightmare world. 3. Experiences of alienation – of being up against it in a relationship from which one cannot get away . . .[30]

Along similar lines Robert Short affirms:

> When we see through the outward, parabolic form in which the New Testament mentions 'hell', we can see that it's talking about the reality of a 'judgment' that occurs in the present, in this lifetime, inside our hearts . . . Even if the wicked never end up in hell, that doesn't mean that in the meantime hell won't be in them.[31]

Hebblethwaite also supports the view 'that hell and eternal punishment are also figurative and symbolic notions, and do not literally describe permanent aspects of reality in the final consummation of the divine purpose'.[32]

30. John Robinson, *But That I Can't Believe!* (Collins, 1967), p.48.
31. Short, *The Gospel from Outer Space*, p.79.
32. Hebblethwaite, *Evil, Suffering and Religion*, p.102.

Paul Tillich sees 'heaven' and 'hell' as 'symbols of ultimate meaning and unconditional significance. But no such threat or promise is made about other than human life'.[33] Tillich goes on to describe heaven and hell as 'symbols and not descriptions of localities' which

> point to the objective basis of blessedness and despair, i.e. the amount of fulfilment or non-fulfilment which goes into the individual's essentialization. The symbols must be taken seriously . . . and can be used as metaphors for the polar ultimates in the experience of the divine.[34]

This hermeneutical approach is governed by a strong existentialist philosophy which is hostile to the revealed truth of Scripture.

The ethical objection to the orthodox doctrine of hell is more well-known. 'If God sends sinners to hell,' people claim, 'then He is cruel and immoral.' Hebblethwaite, representative of many contemporary scholars, insists that 'morally speaking, the idea of eternal punishment has to be rejected by the sensitive moral conscience quite independently of religion'.[35]

We need to note all these contemporary objections carefully and counter them in our churches if we are to communicate the whole counsel of God in a relevant and meaningful way. A great deal of work still needs to be done in this area if we are to teach the truth effectively today.

33. Tillich, *Systematic Theology*, vol.3, p.326.
34. ibid., p.446.
35. Hebblethwaite, *Evil, Suffering and Religion*, p.102.

3
Another Alternative to Hell
Universalism

Another theory seriously undermining the biblical gospel today is universalism. In this chapter, therefore, the development of this increasingly popular theory will be presented.

Definition

The term 'universalism' is used in two conflicting ways. First of all, it is used by orthodox Christians and theologians to describe the worldwide dimension of God's purposes in which sinners from all nations and languages are 'called ... into fellowship with his Son, Jesus Christ our Lord' (1 Cor. 1:9, NIV; Rev. 7:9-10). Salvation is not confined to the Jews nor to the Western world, but includes Jews and Gentiles drawn from all nations (Rom. 10:12-13; 11:11-25; Gal. 3:28; etc.). This does not imply that everyone will be saved, not even ultimately, but rather that heaven will be populated by redeemed sinners from all nations.

Secondly, the term 'universalism' is used to refer to the belief or hope that the whole of humanity will be saved, eventually if not immediately. There are many variations of the theory, and its history, as Richard J. Bauckham reminds us, is indeed 'a complex one'.[1]

Universalism: its earliest history

Origen (c. AD 185-254) stands out in the Patristic period as the most articulate and influential proponent of universalism. He based his theory on a gradual, almost eternal,

1. *Themelios*, vol. 4:2, January 1979, p.48.

process of restoration both for demons and humans. This in turn was undergirded by the fact that God's goodness, which Origen believed always had a remedial, not punitive, purpose in view, aims for the final restoration of all fallen angels and humans to God.

Augustine (AD 354-430) refuted universalism powerfully and persuasively, and his refutation resulted eventually in the condemnation of Origen's universalism by the Council of Constantinople II in AD 553. With only a few exceptions, universalism was effectively removed from the church until the sixteenth-century Protestant Reformation when some radical Anabaptists and Spiritualists popularized the theory. Once again, however, universalism was rejected by churches. Although there were some advocates of universalism in seventeenth-century Europe and America, it was not until the late eighteenth and nineteenth centuries that the theory began to influence Christendom extensively and radically.

F.D.E. Schleiermacher (1768-1834) is the father of modern universalism and his influence on theology has been enormous. For Schleiermacher, the necessity of universal salvation arose from God's free and pure love. This, in turn, was supported by the claim that heaven would not be bliss or even bearable for believers if they were aware of the sufferings of unbelievers in hell. The floodgates were now opened and, by the end of the nineteenth century, 'men were no longer deprived of office for teaching a tentative universalism'.[2]

Universalism in the Twentieth Century

It is during the last three decades that universalism has been articulated and become extremely influential, even militant, within contemporary theology and missiology. We can liken the teaching of universalism during the present

2. Rowell, *Hell and the Victorians*, p.212.

century to a small river meandering through the country-side. The water-level of the river is low although it had risen sharply on occasions. Suddenly, however, due to continuous and exceptionally heavy rains, the water-level rises dangerously before eventually overflowing the river banks and flooding the surrounding countryside. The twentieth century, therefore, is a century of contrasts as far as the history of universalim is concerned. Generally speaking, for the first sixty years universalism was gener-ally assumed, implied and preached but it was not articu-lated theologically nor was it militant until after the mid-sixties when this river burst its banks.

a) *1900-1960s*

There is no need to monitor the progress of liberalism or the tensions between liberalism and evangelicalism or the progress of missionary work in these early decades. While Ernst Troeltsch (1865-1923), Wilfred Cantwell Smith (1916-1973), Hendrik Kraemer (1888-1965), the mission-ary A.G. Hogg and many others wrestled and sympathized with universalism, the influence of Karl Barth and Paul Tillich was dominant. Opinion is divided as to whether or not Barth was a universalist. Universalism is at least implicit in Barth's theology, for he views God's covenant of grace extending to the whole of mankind. For Barth the main difference between believers and unbelievers is that believers know they have been reconciled to God through Christ whereas unbelievers have yet to realize it.

Paul Tillich's theology was even more devastating than Barth's. Certainly Tillich's universalism had a distinctive flavour about it as he reduced Christian doctrines to 'sym-bols' and then spoke of the 'spiritual reality' or 'God' who is in the depths of every living faith.

b) *1960s onwards*

Vatican II (1962-1965) marked a major change by the

Roman Catholic Church of its traditional dogma, 'no salvation outside the church'. The Council affirmed that whatever was pure and true in other religions reflected 'a ray of that Truth which enlightens all men'. Another quotation from Vatican II illustrates the same point:

> Those can also attain to everlasting salvation who, through no fault of their own do not know the gospel of Christ or His church yet sincerely seek God and, moved by His grace, strive by their deeds to do His will as it is known to them through the dictates of conscience. Nor does divine Providence deny the help necessary for salvation to those who, without blame on their part, have not yet arrived at an explicit knowledge of God but strive to live a good life, thanks to His grace.[3]

Several Catholic theologians have taught that other world religions are complementary rather than opposed to Christianity: they include Raymond Pannikar, Karl Rahner and Hans Küng. Pannikar claimed that Christ is present incognito in Hinduism while Rahner developed this thesis more radically, claiming that members of other religions should be regarded as anonymous Christians. Such people, insists Rahner, have an implicit faith although unaware that it is related to Christ. Similarly, a famous distinction is made by Hans Küng between the 'ordinary' way of salvation in world religions and the 'extraordinary' way in the church.

Here is a radically different stance towards people outside the church and it opens the door wide for universalism. Between the creation of the Vatican Secretariat for Non-Christian Religions in May 1964 during the Vatican Council and the issuing of the papal encyclical *Redemptor Hominis* by Pope John Paul II in March 1979, Roman Catholic mission theology underwent a more radical

3. *Lumen Gentium* (Costello Publishing Company, 1984). Vatican Council II, vol. 1, p.16.

change than in any other period, at least during the past century. In his encyclical, the Pope affirmed: 'Every human person without exception has been redeemed by Christ: because Christ is in a way united to the human person – every human person . . . even if the individual may not realize the fact . . .' This encyclical is generally regarded as one of the most significant Roman Catholic doctrinal statements on missiology since Vatican II. The Pope here agrees with Karl Rahner and others who also insisted on the redemptive presence of Jesus Christ extending to the entire human race. Redemption has been accomplished for all people because mankind is united with Christ and redeemed by virtue of the incarnation.

On the Protestant side, the starting-point for this second phase can be dated in 1966. John Hick observes that the approach by Protestant churches to dialogue was dominant within the World Council of Churches until the end of the General Secretaryship of Dr Visser't Hooft in 1966. This approach was based on their Trinitarian confessions of faith. Until that year, there had been no inter-religion dialogue at all. After 1966, dialogue with other religions began but on a confessional Christian basis. Another significant date in the 1960s was 1961 when the WCC held its third Assembly in New Delhi and referred to dialogue as a form of evangelism. A meeting of directors of centres for the study of non-Christian Religions in Asia had been convened earlier that year and a series of consultations were held in the Near East, India, Burma and Hong Kong. The year 1961, then, was also an important milestone.

We need now to mention some of the factors which contributed to the flowering of universalism and the flooding of Christendom by universalism from the 1960s onwards. These factors in themselves are complex and can only be referred to briefly.

A large immigrant community in Britain and Western Europe influenced churches in their attitude to world religions. There is now a new awareness of these religions. For example, there are nearly two million Muslims in Britain now and over 400,000 Hindus. The largest Hindu city in the world outside India or South Africa is Leicester. There are also over 200,000 Sikhs who come either from the Punjab or East Africa. The Jewish Board of Deputies estimates a community figure of over 412,000 Jews in Britain. It is not easy to establish the number of Buddhists who live in Great Britain. Recently, the Chiswick Vihara had a contact list of 20,000 but this excludes the Vietnamese boat people, many of whom are Buddhists; in addition, the second largest ethnic minority here is the Chinese community for whom Buddhism is the dominant philosophy. There are also groups of Zoroastrians and Jains. The Baha'i community has nearly two hundred assemblies in Britain with several thousand members.

Do they all worship the same God? Will these people be saved even if they never believe on Christ? Can we regard their sacred books as legitimate revelations of the One Being and their leaders as having the same authority and status as Christ? These are the crucial questions forced upon churches since the mid-sixties. It was only in November 1977 that the British Council of Churches called on its members to affirm that 'we recognize that Great Britain is now a pluralist society of varied races, cultures and religions; we must respect those who practise different religions . . .' There is, however, a wider dimension to the problem. Hans Küng reminds us that we are 'en route to a global ecumenical consciousness'.[4] Out of approximately five billion people living on the earth, only 1.5 billion are nominal Christians. This compares with between 800-900 million Muslims, 583 million Hindus and 274 million Buddhists. Will over two-thirds of the world's population be damned? Basic facts like these have made many church

4. Hans Küng, *Christianity and the World Religions*, Fount Paperbacks (Collins, 1987), p.13.

leaders and theologians question the unique claims of Christianity and advocate instead a dogmatic universalism.

There are other factors, too. A militant Islam in the West, the popularity of Eastern religions in Europe and North America, the influence of comparative studies of religion in schools/colleges and facilities for travel as well as the general philosophical and theological climate are further influences which have served to bring into the centre of theological and missiological thinking the crucial question of Christ's lordship over a world that is religiously plural. In this context, John Hick claims 'we are living at a turning point in the history of Christianity'.[5]

Among those who adopt an inclusive universalist position regarding world religions, there are two main approaches. Firstly, there is a *Christological approach*, and, secondly, there is a *radical/relative 'God-centred' approach*. Both approaches will be outlined in this chapter. The former expresses sympathy or support for universalism in a Christological and, at times, Trinitarian context, whereas the latter demotes Jesus Christ to one of several world religious teachers and so argues the need to go beyond Christ or Mohammed to 'God' who is common to all religions.

1. Christological approach

Barth's theology continued to exercise a powerful influence in the 1960s and early 1970s. This influence can be traced in numerous directions but, in particular, in relation to individual scholars/writers like William Barclay, W.A. Visser't Hooft, T.F. Torrance, Lesslie Newbigin, etc. and also the early theological reflection within the World Council of Churches. The Fatherhood of God was a key in the developing theology of William Barclay (1907-78) and in his later years he embraced universalism on the ground that the divine love is Christologically orientated but

5. John Hick, *The Second Christianity* (SCM, 1983), p.9.

embraces the whole of mankind. Visser't Hooft (1900-85), a dominant leader and influence in the World Council of Churches, combined a deep sympathy towards world religions with a strong Christological base. Lesslie Newbigin adopts a similar approach:

> In the coming of Christ, his dying, rising and ascension, is the decisive moment in God's plan of salvation . . . [it is] not implied that the vast multitudes who have never been presented with this Gospel . . . are thereby necessarily excluded from participation in God's on-going and completed work.[6]

Due to his active participation in the work of the WCC, Barth also influenced its early theology and methodology from 1955 to 1982. The slow acceleration of interest in pluralism on the part of the WCC, especially from 1948 to 1966, may have been due to Barth's influence. By the Fifth WCC Assembly in Nairobi in 1975, there had been significant changes in the attitude of the WCC towards other religions. This was the first assembly to which persons of other faiths were officially invited as guests; the debate on this subject was framed in terms of the 'community of all humanity'. The Christological approach was now losing favour within ecumenical circles.

The major Christological approach to religious pluralism, however, was to be seen on the Roman Catholic side in the writings, for example, of Raymond Pannikar, Karl Rahner and Hans Küng.

Born in 1918, Pannikar was the son of a Hindu father and a Spanish Roman Catholic mother. He himself became a Roman Catholic priest and worked in India for many years. Later, he was appointed Professor of Religious Studies at the University of California. His famous book, *The Unknown Christ of Hinduism*, was published in 1968 and made an immediate impact on Christendom. For Pannikar,

6. Lesslie Newbigin, *The Finality of Christ* (London, 1969), p.61.

both Christianity and Hinduism meet in Christ. Hindu knowledge is defective for it teaches that people only meet in the Absolute at the end of their pilgrimage. Christians are able to spell out this meeting place as being in Christ for there is only one mediator between God and humans. Behind all prayers, encounters and revelations, whether Hindu or Christian, stands Christ. He is the 'light of the world' in this sense (John 1:1-9). Christ is present incognito, therefore, in Hinduism and at work in Hindu worship and experience. Rather than describe it as a false religion, Pannikar sees Hinduism as 'a vestibule of Christianity'.

Karl Rahner was a theological consultant in Vatican II and played a major role in the official reinterpretation of the traditional Roman dogma that there is no salvation outside the Church. In his *Christianity and Non-Christian Religions*,[7] Rahner expounds three theses which are fundamental to his theology of religions. The first is that Christianity understands itself to be the absolute religion for all mankind. The second thesis is that a non-Christian religion contains elements flowing out of divine grace gratuitously given on account of Christ. For this reason, other religions can, in different degrees, be recognized as lawful religions without denying the errors in them. The third thesis is that members of extra-Christian religions must be regarded as *anonymous Christians*: such people have an implicit faith although unaware that it is related to Christ.

Rahner's theology is open, of course, to serious criticism. John Hick describes it as 'an honorary status granted unilaterally to people who have not expressed any desire for it'.[8] Hans Küng is also critical, claiming that the idea of 'anonymous Christians' is offensive to non-Christians and also that it pre-empts dialogue without facing up to the challenge of world religions. Sir Norman Anderson

7. These were lectures he delivered in Bavaria just prior to the opening of Vatican II in 1962. The book was published in 1980 by Fount.
8. John Hick, *God Has Many Names* (Macmillan, 1980), p.50f.

also rejects Rahner's concept of an 'anonymous Christian'.[9]

Hans Küng must now be mentioned briefly. Küng is a Swiss Roman Catholic theologian who has taught in Tübingen since 1960. For his radical views and questioning of Roman Catholic dogma (e.g. papal infallibility), Küng was deprived in 1979 of his licence to teach as a Roman Catholic theologian. Some of Küng's better-known works include *Justification* (1965), *The Church* (1967), *Infallible?* (1971), *On Being a Christian* (1977) and *Eternal Life* (1984).

Küng's theology is certainly not orthodox. Even his doctrine of Christ is defective for he constructs the historical Jesus from critical studies and rejects the Chalcedon formula of Jesus being true man and true God. Küng refuses to say more than the vague statement: 'God in Jesus Christ'. Küng's unorthodoxy is further seen in his attitude towards other religions:

> A man is to be saved within the religion that is made available to him in his historical situation. Hence it is his right and duty to seek God within that religion . . . The religions . . . are the . . . general . . . 'ORDINARY' way of salvation, as against which the way of salvation in the church appears as something very special and extra-ordinary.[10]

In a more recent book,[11] Küng enters into dialogue with Islam, Hinduism and Buddhism. In his response to Islam, Küng spends time discussing the crucial difference in their understanding of the Person of Jesus.[12] Was He God the Son? Or was He only a man? His disturbing answer is that

9. Sir Norman Anderson, *Christianity and World Religions* (IVP, 1984), p.172f.
10. Hans Küng, *Christian Revelation and World Religions* (London: J. Neuner, 1967), p.52ff.
11. Hans Küng, *Christianity and the World Religions* (1987).
12. ibid., pp.116-30.

the historical person of Jesus Christ only 'represents', 'manifests' and 'definitely reveals' God but Christ was not God! Any criticism of Küng's universalism must expose his unbiblical assumptions and methodology.

2. Radical God-centred approach

Another strand of universalism is even more devastating and this is what I call the radical/relative 'God-centred' approach. It is this radical approach which will concern us in the rest of this chapter.

Richard J. Bauckman asserts that 'two of the most per-suasive of recent arguments for dogmatic universalism' are those of John T. Robinson (1919-1983) and John Hick.[13] Like Hick, Robinson's main argument concerns God's omnipotent love; it is this divine love which elicits from all people eventually a willing submission and acceptance.[14] We shall not consider in detail Robinson's teaching but concentrate on Hick who is a prolific writer on the subject of Christianity and World Religions. In 1968 he published his *Christianity at the Centre* (a second edition was pub-lished in 1977 and later issued in 1983 as *The Second Christianity*) and, a little later, *Evil and the God of Love*. In the latter especially, Hick concluded that Christians must uphold the ultimate salvation of all God's creatures. Sup-port for this conclusion came in his *God and the Universe of Faiths* (1973) in which he advocated the need for a 'Copernican revolution' in the theology of religion; this involves a shift from a Christ-centred to a God-centred model of the universe of faiths. If Hick was to achieve this, then the orthodox, literal doctrine of the Person of Christ had to be undermined and the debate re-opened. This was achieved with *The Myth of God Incarnate* published in 1977. The book was a collection of essays by seven British

13. *Themelios*, vol. 4:2, January 1979, p.53.
14. An excellent summary of Robinson's theology is provided by Alistair Kee in *The Roots of Christian Freedom: The Theology of John Robinson* (SPCK, 1988), pp.113-20.

theologians and edited by Hick; he also wrote the concluding essay, 'Jesus and the World Religions'. Here Hick
rejects the traditional Christology of Chalcedon and Nicea
as 'mythical . . . traditional language'. According to Hick,
Jesus had been 'deified' by the early church. Do we appreciate, therefore, the setting of the 'Myth of God' debate and
the way it was deliberately 'staged' in order to undermine
biblical theology?

By 1980, Hick's views were well-developed and expressed in another book entitled *God Has Many Names*.[15] Here
he takes even further his forceful argument that the universe of faiths must centre upon God, not upon Christianity or any other religion. Hick uses two main arguments
in support of his unbiblical position.

1. 'God' alone is at the centre of all religions, including Christianity

A proper study and appreciation of Jesus, according to
Hick, demands that close attention be given to the God in
whom He believed. 'God was so completely real to him that
it is impossible to think of him without this consciousness
of God.'[16] This 'Transcendental Reality' is not, in Hick's
view, confined to the Christian religion but it opens up a
'global theology' of religions in general.

Hick illustrates the point in two ways. First of all, while
'the trappings are different' and God is described differently, yet what is done in all religions is 'essentially the
same'.[17] Secondly, Hick attempts to show that different
religions have the same basic beliefs about God. Are the
different names used by various religions for God only differences in name or do they refer to different gods? Hick
insists that the one, transcendent God is common to all
religions, but as the transcendent One is infinite, it is

15. John Hick, *God Has Many Names* (Macmillan, 1980).
16. John Hick, *The Second Christianity* (SCM, 1983), p.35.
17. *God Has Many Names*, p.45.

impossible to describe and conceptualize Him in any unique or authoritative way. This argument is undergirded for Hick and others by the thought of the unity of all mankind before God.[18] This in turn necessitates the affirmation of God's equal love for all and also the acknowledgment that a single revelation to the whole earth 'has never in the past been possible'.[19] Wesley Ariarajah has also popularized this viewpoint as director of the Dialogue Sub-unit of the WCC.[20] Archbishop Robert Runcie has also given expression to it in several addresses in recent years. Not only is mankind one, declares Runcie, but 'if God is merciful to any he will be merciful to all'.[21] Another key address of Runcie's was entitled 'Meeting of Faiths' in which he adopts a position almost akin to that of Hick. Speaking of God, Dr Runcie writes:

> This irreducible mystery can only be reverently approached in prayer, meditation and praise; it often finds a powerful symbolic expression in many of our places of worship and shrines, whether they be Hindu, Moslem, Sikh, Buddhist or Christian.[22]

To return to Hick's basic thesis that there is one transcendent God common to all religions, there are several criticisms to be made. First of all, his historial argument is suspect. Following Jaspers' designation of the sixth-seventh centuries BC as the 'axial' period in the history of religions, Hick argues there was an upsurge of religious encounters/insights in this period. These came to be expressed in distinct religious patterns or religions, largely due to geographic isolation. But Christianity and Islam did not originate in the axial period and some religions were in

18. This is a common argument; see, e.g. *The Unity of the Church and the Unity of Mankind* (Faith & Order, 1969).
19. Hick, *God Has Many Names*, p.74.
20. Wesley Ariarajah, *The Bible and People of Other Faiths* (WCC, 1987).
21. Robert Runcie, *One Light for One World* (SPCK, 1988), p.59.
22. ibid., p.191.

close contact with and not isolation from one another.[23]

Secondly, Hick's theology is unacceptable. For example, he advocates an unadulterated liberalism; he rejects the God revealed in the Bible, whose wrath and judgment are inextricably related to, and are expressions of, the essential holiness of His Being. He also refuses to acknowledge the uniqueness and inerrancy of the Bible, insisting that religious truth cannot be expressed in words or concepts. But why not? Here Hick is exposing his own secular presuppositions which are assumed rather than argued in his works.

One must also question the claim that the same transcendent God is common to all religions. For Hick, God is a personal being with a mind and will; he is the Creator and Lord of the universe. But not all religions agree with this description of God: for example, the Vedantist Hindu or the Therevada Buddhist. Muslims and Christians, too, have radically different concepts of God.

2. The denial of the unique Person of Christ

Hick's view of Christ is clear but distressing; Jesus of Nazareth was no more than a man who had a deep consciousness of, and submission to, God. In support of this denial, Hick uses the following arguments:

a) *Critical studies of the New Testament*

Agreeing with critics of the New Testament, Hick insists there are different and conflicting Christologies within the New Testament and even questions the resurrection narratives but admits 'some kind of experience of seeing Jesus after his death'.[24] The claim to deity, therefore, is part of the 'mythical' structure of the New Testament; its true meaning is not literal but poetic and symbolic. This argument is really a rehash of what other critics have said for

23. *Themelios*, vol. 9:2, p.17.
24. Hick, *God Has Many Names*, p.62.

decades and it provides another example of Hick's liberal, critical approach to Scripture and his denial of the supernatural.

b) *Early Christology is relative, not normative, being the result of conjecture and speculation by Christians; this process culminated in the classical definitions of Chalcedon and Nicea*

Hick thinks he knows how the process of deification of Christ developed. As Jesus made an impact upon the lives of people, Hick suggests, then there was pressure to use the highest titles to describe His person and work. For over a thousand years the 'symbols' of Jesus, he suggests, as 'Son of God' and 'Logos' made flesh, served their purpose well, although they came to be understood literally not symbolically. More recently, with the dawn of biblical criticism and now greater interaction between peoples and religions, the literal interpretation has been in disfavour.

By way of reply, I confine myself to a helpful statement by Gerald Bray:

> The line of development from the teaching of Jesus to the creeds of the church was not a deviation from the original intention of Christ . . . it was the logical response to the question which Jesus asked His disciples in Matthew 16:15. The entire achievement of early Christian theology can be explained as an answer to this question – the answer which alone makes sense of the New Testament and gives an adequate explanation for the later progress and triumph of Christianity.[25]

c) *The nature of religious language*

Hick takes the statement, 'Jesus was God the Son incarnate' and asks: is its meaning literal, symbolic, mythological or poetic? He concludes it is meaningless to say Jesus

25. Gerald Bray, *Creeds, Councils and Christ* (IVP, 1984), p.71.

is literally God. But why? He replies that saying Jesus is both man *and* God is like saying a circle is a square![26] However, this is unfair and one wonders whether Hick understands what the creeds teach about our Lord. They do not teach that God is man but rather that God the Son has a divine nature and, from the incarnation, a human nature, yet both are 'preserved' and united in the unity of His divine Person. He is truly God and truly man in one Person but Hick's reductionist methodology interprets the doctrine as only expressing a subjective valuation and evoking an attitude.

26. Hick, *God Has Many Names*, p.71.

4
Universalism
A Biblical Assessment

Having traced in the previous chapter the development of universalism, we will here consider the Bible passages which are used extensively by some contemporary writers in support of universalism and Christ's salvific relationship to the whole of mankind. Five passages will be examined, namely, John 1:1; Acts 17:23; Ephesians 1:10; Colossians 1:15; and 1 Corinthians 15:24-28.

1. Christ as logos in John 1:1

From the early Christian apologist, Justin Martyr, to contemporary theologians like Karl Rahner, Hans Küng and John Hick, etc., the term *logos* has been used to justify the view that Christ is present in all religions and philosophies, albeit in a somewhat hidden way.

John Hick writes, 'If we call God-acting-towards-mankind the Logos then we must say that ALL salvation, within all religions, is the work of the Logos.[1]

Our exegesis, therefore, must be provided within the framework of:

a) the background, b) the context, and c) the definition of Logos in John 1:1.

a) *The background*

Frequently it is claimed that John's employment of the term *logos* is a deliberate and justifiable attempt to syncretize Greek concepts with Christian dogma. Tillich would say that this is part of essential Christian 'universality' in

1. Hick, *God Has Many Names*, p.75.

which dogma interacts continuously with secular and pagan religious thought.

But what is the background to the Logos? The usual reply is to assume that its background and meaning are dominantly Greek. Let us pause and consider this briefly.

Certainly there is a Greek background to the concept of Logos. Heraclitus thought of it as a principle or Law, Reason unifying matter in a changing world; for Anaxagoras Logos mediated between a transcendent God and the world; the Stoics taught that ethereal fire was the original source of all things and was known as *logos spermatikos*, i.e. Seminal Reason, but conceived in the plural; and Philo, influenced by Greek thought, developed the Logos idea as something impersonal, pre-existent and mediated between the transcendent God and the world.

However, and contrary to what Rahner and others assume, 'there has been a definite shift of emphasis from Greek to Hebrew sources for the interpretation of the fourth gospel as a whole', writes Donald Guthrie, 'and this applies to the prologue in particular'.[2] These Jewish sources include the Old Testament background (creative Word of God in Genesis 1; Psalm 33:6-9; a sustaining providential care through the Word: Psalms 147:15-18; 148:8; the Word as the means of revelation: Jeremiah 20:9; Ezekiel 33:7; etc.), the wisdom literature, the rabbinic idea of the Torah and the Qumran literature. It is this Jewish Old Testament background in particular which dominates the Johannine usage of *logos*. John 1:1, therefore, is not evidence of a syncretistic use of Greek philosophy. There are radical differences, for example, between Philo's Logos and the Logos of John 1:1. One major difference is that the divine Logos (John 1) is personal and pre-existent. Furthermore, Philo's Greek philosophy would not

2. Donald Guthrie, *New Testament Theology* (Inter-Varsity Press, 1981), pp.323-4.

allow the Logos to be incarnate (1:14) in an evil, material world.

b) *The context*

Contextual factors are also of crucial importance in exegeting John 1:1-14. Some theologians talk of 'the non-incarnate Christ' or Logos, while Hick impersonalizes the Logos to some extent by describing Logos vaguely as 'God-in-relation-to-man'. Also, Karl Barth believes that John 1:1ff 'contains self-evidently' the truth that Jesus Christ is the elected man! One cannot but agree with Colin Brown that this is 'wholly lacking in these verses'.[3] Note, therefore, in the context that the Lord Jesus Christ is described in a three-fold relationship:

i.   to the Father, v.1;
ii. to the world, vv.3-10;
iii. to people, vv.11-14.

As our subject of universalism in its contemporary expression touches on and misunderstands each of these three relationships, we need briefly to summarize the teaching here.

i. In relation to the Father, Christ is identified in verse 1:
     as pre-existent: *en archē;*
     as having personality and in the closest fellowship
        with the Father: *pros ton Theon;*
     as divine: *Theos ēn ho logos.*

Notice that the imperfect indicative, 'was', is used in all three clauses, expressing each time 'continuous timeless existence'.[4] Verse two underlines the fact that this relationship with the Father was eternal and intimate.

ii. In relation to the world, verses 3ff.

Christ is the creator of all things and all peoples. In verse

3. C. Brown, *Karl Barth and the Christian Message* (Tyndale, 1967), p.107.
4. J. H. Bernard, *International Critical Commentary* (T. & T. Clark, 1928), vol.1, p.cxxxviii ff.

3, Greek/Gnostic ideas (i.e. that matter is eternal and that angels were used in creating the world) are contradicted. Christ Himself, and only Christ, is responsible for creation, yet He must not be identified with the creation (i.e. pantheism). Two different verbs are used: with regard to the Logos, 'to be', and with regard to the creation, 'to become'.

Verse 4 includes two crucial statements.

Firstly, 'in him was life'. The preposition here is 'in', not 'through', thus stressing that life has always resided in the Word. 'Life' here cannot mean physical life for, as God, the Word is spirit. Once again the immediate context helps us to interpret the word 'life'. For example, in the rest of verse 4, the 'life' is described as the 'light of men'; in verse 5, this light shines into the darkness without having been overcome by it. Although there are other ways of translating *katelaben*, it is best understood as a reference to the continuous display of the light in the world of humans; light which has not been extinguished. Later, in verses 7-9, John came to bear witness to this light. This 'light' is therefore spiritual, not physical and is inseparably related to, and even identified with, Christ.

In the Johannine writings, 'life' and 'light' are related and have a strong spiritual connotation. Hendriksen argues that 'life' refers to 'the fulness of God's essence'[5] and yet is the cause and preserver of all physical and spiritual life.

Secondly, 'that life was the light of men'. How are we to interpret the rest of verse 4? With the fact of creation mentioned in verse 3, 'men' referred to comprehensively in verse 4 and the Fall at least implied in verse 5, the 'light of men' refers to the general revelation of God in His creation. This revelation has been stamped upon creation; it is true, but general and insufficient for it does not reveal the mercy and salvation of God. Into this world the Logos came with

5. William Hendriksen, *The Gospel of John* (Banner of Truth, 1959), i, p.72.

a fulness of light but with an essentially redemptive purpose. Contrary to what is taught by Rahner, Küng and Hick etc., there is no redemptive or salvific function for general revelation. Neither the unity of mankind, the fact of general revelation nor the divine attribute of love makes the incarnation and redemptive mission of Christ unnecessary or 'symbolic'. The Prologue makes this clear.

iii. In relation to the people, verse 14.

The Prologue climaxes in 1:14. Here is a historical event of the utmost significance for the world. It is appropriate to refer here to verse 9. The verse can be interpreted in two ways: is it the light (Christ) that is coming into the world, or the light every person has when he is born? There are good arguments for both interpretations, but if the second alternative is chosen (i.e. the light of general revelation), then this would not be the light of salvation as some are arguing. Christ enlightens people in creation in the sense that He created them in the image of God. The whole context and climax of verse 4 forbid the inclusion of light in any salfivic sense.

c) *Definition and use of Logos, John 1:1*

It is not easy to translate the Greek *logos* because of its associations, but it is preferable to retain the translation 'Word' here, although it has its weaknesses. In the Greek, the noun originally came from *legein*, 'to say', suggesting the utterance of an important statement in contrast to ordinary talk and conversation (*lalein*). Against the Old Testament background of the Word revealing and accomplishing God's utterance, John displays the glory of Christ in the Prologue as God and the Logos thus qualified to reveal God to the world. He is further described as the revealer of God in 1:18. In between verses 1 and 18, it is sometimes claimed with some justification that the passage concentrates on the method of revelation rather than the person and qualifications of the Logos who reveals.

What is the apostle's purpose in describing Christ as the Logos in the Prologue? He is certainly not super-imposing a 'mythical' or philosophical framework upon Jesus of Nazareth as some suggest. Rather, John proceeds in the Gospel to further describe Jesus Christ, the Logos, as the Son of God and this is confirmed in John 20:31. Donald Guthrie suggests in a helpful way that:

> The Christology of the gospel, with its combination of true humanity with divine nature, was expressed in contemporary terms with a view to offsetting the docetic-type over-emphasis on the divine at the expense of the human, a real danger to the stability of the early Christian Christology. A Logos doctrine on its own might have been construed to support the docetic notion, but in connection with the rest of the gospel, which stresses even more clearly than the synoptics the human characteristic of Jesus, the 'becoming flesh' becomes diametrically opposed to docetism.[6]

2. Paul's statement in Acts 17:23

F.F. Bruce remarks that 'probably no ten verses in the Acts have formed the text for such an abundance of commentary ...'.[7] In this passage, Paul is speaking before the Areopagus in Athens and it is an example of his method of addressing a pagan, intellectual, but superstitious audience.

In verse 22, is Paul being derogatory or making a plain statement of fact about Athenian religious life? 'Then Paul stood in the midst of Mars' hill, and said, Ye men of Athens, I perceive that in all things ye are too superstitious.' To answer the question, we need to look at the Greek word translated 'superstitious' (AV) or 'religious'

6. Guthrie, *New Testament Theology*, p.329.
7. F.F. Bruce, *Acts*, The New London Commentary (Marshall, Morgan & Scott, 1956), p.353.

(NIV). The Abbot-Smith lexicon defines the word as meaning 'reverent to the deity, religious'. Admittedly it is a general word with some elasticity of meaning, but it is not used by Paul in a derogatory manner. The Athenians were unusually religious and devoted to many kinds of gods. There were shrines and gods all over the city, both in public and private places. Paul, therefore, is stating a fact when he describes them as being very religious or devoted to gods.

Despite all their religion and 'objects of worship' (v.23), the Athenians did not know the true God. Paul then refers to an altar he had found with the inscription, 'UNKNOWN GOD'. Jerome suggested that Paul is referring collectively to the 'gods' of the city under the singular form. This inscription provides the apostle with his point of contact, for he then proceeds to tell them about the one, true God.

The statement in verse 23 is an important corrective to contemporary universalism. 'For as I passed by, and beheld your devotions, I found an altar with this inscription, TO THE UNKNOWN GOD. Whom therefore ye ignorantly worship, him declare I unto you.' Their inscription confirmed the fact that they were ignorant (*agnoountes* – to be ignorant, not to know) of the character and message of God; so Paul tells them about Him. What is underlined here is their ignorance of the true God. Today, by contrast, universalists infer from the fact of sincere worship in all religions that people are thereby worshipping the one, transcendent God. Such a belief is not taught or implied here. In fact, Howard Marshall claims that Paul's words here 'at least to Jewish readers would have a derogatory nuance . . . there is no real connection between an "unknown God" and the true God. Paul hardly meant that his audience were unconscious worshippers of the true God'.[8]

From verse 24 Paul tells them about the only God, the

8. Howard Marshall, *Acts* (Tyndale, 1980), p.285.

creator Lord of the universe, independent yet supplying the needs of people and giving them the whole earth for habitation. 'God that made the world and all things therein, seeing that he is Lord of heaven and earth, dwelleth not in temples made with hands; neither is worshipped with men's hands, as though he needed any thing, seeing he giveth to all life, and breath, and all things; and hath made of one blood all nations of men for to dwell on all the face of the earth, and hath determined the times before appointed, and the bounds of their habitation.'

According to verse 25, God does not require anything from His creatures; in fact, He it is who supplies all that they have, including their life and breath. Verse 26 is also rich in teaching and three truths are taught here. First, all humans have been created by God, and, therefore, all men are equal before Him. 'It was the boast of the Athenians', writes E.M. Blaiklock, 'that they had "sprung from the soil". The truth Paul put into these words cut at the root of all national pride, engendered by polytheism on the one hand and philosophic pride on the other. The Stoic, especially Seneca and Epictetus, had glimpsed the truth of the unity of mankind under God, but such philosophy lacked "a lifting power". . . It was not given to the Greek or to the Roman, but to the Jew, separated though he was from every other nation, to safeguard the truth of the unity of mankind . . .'.[9] The second truth taught in verse 26 is that God, in addition to creating the entire human race, has given people the whole earth to live in. Thirdly, the verse illustrates God's sovereign control of the world: 'and hath determined the times before appointed, and the bounds of their habitation'. National boundaries as well as times are all decreed by God and not by fate or chance.

However, God's creative and providential works have an important purpose and this is expressed at the beginning

9. E. M. Blaiklock, *Acts* (Tyndale, 1959), p.141.

of verse 27. 'That they should seek the Lord, if haply they might feel after him, and find him, though he be not far from every one of us.' What was the divine purpose in arranging times and places for man's well-being? It was 'that they should seek the Lord' and 'feel after him, and find him'. Universalists today claim that the unity of mankind before God also involves automatic salvation for all peoples, whatever their religion, ignorance or sin. In other words, they insist that God's creative and providential works are salvific in nature. But they are wrong and unbiblical at this point. Made in the image of God, and given ample general revelation in creation and providence which points to the existence of a God who is powerful, eternal and sovereign, men are 'without excuse' (Rom. 1:20) if they do not acknowledge, seek and glorify this great God. It is in the context of Romans 1:19ff that we must understand the seeking and feeling after the Lord in Acts 17:27. Such a God is immanent and near to those who seek Him according to His truth. Numerous Greek teachers and poets had seen the futility of housing the divine nature in temples or representing the Deity in images; however imperfectly, they had also perceived that God was near to those who sought Him. It is against the background of general revelation and man's accountability that God 'now commands all men everywhere to repent' (v.30) and to submit to the fuller knowledge of God revealed in the gospel.

3. The 'Cosmic Christ' in Ephesians 1:10 and Colossians 1:15

Universalists argue that there is an implication here that all people will eventually be saved when all things will be brought completely under the Lord's authority. At this point, however, Francis Foulkes replies that 'it is dangerous to press a doctrine from a verse without regard for the balance of Scripture as a whole . . .'[10] Foulkes is right, for Scripture has to be interpreted by Scripture and even the context of these passages makes universalism untenable.

For example, in Ephesians 1:3-14 the apostle is giving praise for God's purpose and rich blessings in Christ towards His people. Only believers are in view here; note especially the words 'in Christ' (v.1c) and the teaching that Christians are chosen (v.4), predestinated (v.5), redeemed and forgiven (v.7) and made recipients of special revelation (vv.8-9) and enjoy the prospect of glory (vv.13-14).

In verse 10, God's sovereign plan is being accomplished in Christ, "that in the dispensation of the fulness of times he might gather together in one all things in Christ, both which are in heaven, and which are on earth; even in him.' These words include a prospective reference to the 'dispensation' (*oikonomia* describes the management of a home or the person responsible for it; the church is God's household) of the fulness of times' (i.e. the appropriate time when the Lord returns). This in turn will involve the revelation of a glorious plan: to 'gather together in one all things in Christ . . .'. The Greek translated 'gather' in the AV is variously translated as 'sum up' (RV), 'unite' (RSV), and is used in Romans 13:9 for the summing up of all the commandments in one commandment of love. The idea of 'bringing together' is prominent with even a suggestion of Christ also 'heading up' all things and this fits in with the apostle's design in 1:10-22, cf. 4:10. This teaching is underlined in 1:20-22. Basically, we are informed that *everything* will have been brought under Christ's rule and the submission of all things to Christ will be achieved and manifested at the end of the world. The ideas of restoration (i.e. glorification for believers and creation), unity and the lordship of Christ are prominent but exclude the possibility that unbelievers will be saved. Such a position contradicts the teaching of the passage and other Scriptures.

10. Francis Foulkes, *Ephesians* (Tyndale, 1963), p.53.

In Colossians 1:15, the Person and work of Christ are inseparably related and described; in verses 15-20 the pre-eminence of the Son is emphasized. Christ is not a mere man; His unique Person must not be questioned for He is supreme over all creation (v.15) and is the agent of creation (v.16) and the purpose for which all things were created. Christ is also eternal (v.17) and by Him the whole creation is preserved. This Lord of creation, however, is also Head of the church. God's purpose is that the Lord Jesus may be pre-eminent in all things.

4. Does 1 Corinthians 15:24-28 teach universalism?

No. To understand the passage we will examine:

a) the theme of the chapter,

b) the immediate context of verse 24,

c) the message of vv.24-28.

a) *the theme of the chapter*

The historicity, centrality and significance of Christ's resurrection are the theme which is developed in the chapter. From verses 20 to 28, the fact and consequences of the Lord's resurrection are underlined with the perspective of the glorious consummation of God's purposes. One reason for writing the chapter is recorded in verse 12c.

b) *the immediate context of verse 24*

After the declaration of verse 20 ('But now is Christ risen from the dead, and become the firstfruits of them that slept') a clear parallel is drawn in verse 21 between Adam and Christ; the parallel assumes the solidarity of all humans in Adam and of the church in Christ. Notice, there are no verbs here and no articles in the nouns. 'For since by man came death, by man came also the resurrection of the dead.' 'For' (*gar*) introduces the explanation of the statement in verse 20c.

In verse 22, Paul changes the preposition from *dia*, verse 21, to *en* to emphasize the sphere in which people are found: 'in Adam . . . in Christ'. The verbs are important, too; 'die' is a frequentative present ('they go on dying', contrasting with the aorist tense in Romans 5:12) expressing the continuous effects of Adam's sin. The future tense is used for 'made alive', thus pointing forward to the resurrection at Christ's *parousia*.

'All' is used twice in verse 22. Does this support universalism? Note:

i. Although the word is used twice and without a modifier, yet, as Lenski observes, no modifier is needed, for Paul is talking predominantly about believers and *their* resurrection.

ii. Scriptures like Romans 5:12-21 confirm the assumption here that the 'all' in Adam refers comprehensively to the entire human race, while the 'all' in relation to Christ refers only to believers.

iii. The verb translated 'made alive' (*zōopoieō*) is never used of unbelievers in the New Testament.

iv. The force of the preposition *en* is important. For example, the phrase 'in Christ' is a technical Pauline expression denoting union with Christ; it is limited to the elect who are effectually called to Christ.

v. Those who 'shall be made alive', verse 22c, are described as those who 'are Christ's' (v.23; the genitive of possession is used here) and 'every man', verse 23, is governed by verse 22c.

vi. In the light of earlier passages like 6:9-11, universalism cannot be implied, either by the twofold use of 'all' in verse 22 or by the closing words of verse 28.

c) *the message of verses 24-28*

Verse 24 begins emphatically but without a verb; 'Then the end' (*telos*), which refers to the parousia of verse 23. The Greek *hotan*, 'when', is used twice here; chronologically the second 'when' precedes the first. To describe Christ's final achievement, the aorist subjunctive is used; 'shall have put down utterly', i.e. all opposition. Only after this happens will Christ 'deliver up [present subjunctive] the kingdom to God, even the Father'. This latter point is elaborated in verse 28. There is no suggestion in verse 24 that Christ no longer rules; rather, He fulfils in His mediatorial lordship and in a glorious way the tasks assigned to Him. It is the work of Christ to destroy all opposition and wickedness.

Verses 25-6 tell us why the Son *must* (*dei gar*) continue His mediatorial rule until death, the last enemy, is destroyed (prophetic present is used). Again, the stress is still on believers.

There are two points to note in verse 27:

i. Paul uses the aorist tense in quoting Psalm 8:6, so here is a past action.

ii. The rest of verse 27 explains that 'all things' cannot include God.

In verse 28, notice:

i. The *success* of Christ; the opening words link with verses 24c, 25c, etc.

ii. The *subjection* of Christ to the Father; how are we to understand this? We will go astray here unless we think of Christ here as the Son *en sarki* (incarnate), the God-man, our Mediator. Until the ascension of Christ, God ruled as God but afterwards He rules through the Mediator to whom He gave all authority in heaven and earth (Matt.

28:18). This universal authority is given to Christ in His office as Mediator for His mediatorial kingship in which He builds, edifies, rules, defends and glorifies the church as well as destroying all enemies. Once this work is completed, 'the Son also himself will be subject to Him ...' (i.e. God the Father). There is now no need for economy of functions within the Godhead because all has been accomplished and now the Triune God rules supreme. Christ continues to rule but does so in the unity of the Three Persons of the Godhead.

iii. The *supremacy* of God; 'that God may be all in all', (*panta en pasin*) (verse 28c). In the light of other scriptures, one must reject the view that pantheism is taught here. Nor is this a restricted reference to the redeemed when God is supreme among them. More is involved, especially in the light of verses 24-28 where everything is brought into submission to Christ. The phrase 'all in all' speaks of completeness and supremacy. Does this suggest that even unbelievers will be saved eventually? No, for this again would contradict the general Bible teaching. Charles Hodge catches the meaning when he writes:

> The passage does not teach us the design of redemption, but what is to happen when the redemption of God's people is accomplished. Then the Messianic reign is to cease, and God is to rule supreme over a universe reduced to order, the people of God being saved, and the finally impenitent shut up with Satan and his angels ...[11]

From this examination of key biblical passages, we conclude that there is no biblical warrant for assuming that Christ is present in all world religions and philosophies nor that the whole of mankind will be saved. In view of Christ's clear teaching concerning the future punishment

11. Charles Hodge, *1 Corinthians* (Banner of Truth, 1958), p.336.

of sinners, universalism must be rejected for it requires us 'not only to revise our view of judgment but also to change our view of the Judge.[12]

---

12. Bruce Milne, *I Want to Know what the Bible says about the End of the World* (Kingsway, 1979), p.117.

5
The Wrath of God

More than one writer has drawn attention to the fact that there are more references in the Bible to the anger and wrath of God than there are to the love of God,[1] and a careful reading of a concordance will quickly confirm this fact. If further evidence is required, we can add that there are in the Old Testament alone over twenty Hebrew words used to describe the wrath of God, and these words are used nearly 600 times. Contrary to popular opinion, the New Testament retains and develops this emphasis, so that one writer claims with justification that 'the Bible could be called the book of God's wrath, for it is full of portrayals of divine retribution, from the cursing and banishment of Adam and Eve in Genesis 3 to the overthrow of "Babylon" and the great assizes of Revelation'.[2]

Besides defining the wrath of God in this chapter, we shall investigate biblical examples of God's wrath in action before finally considering some difficulties in relation to this doctrine.

A definition

The attribute of wrath describes *the controlled and permanent opposition of God's holy nature to all sin.* Such abhorrence of sin on God's part is not a whim or a mere decision of the will, nor is it uncontrolled temper or capriciousness, as some imagine, but the reaction of His glorious and perfect nature to sin. For this reason, wrath is as basic to the divine nature as is love; and without wrath God would cease to be God.

1. One example is A.W. Pink, *The Attributes of God* (Baker, 1975), p.97.
2. J. I. Packer, *Knowing God* (Hodder & Stoughton, 1973), p.166.

Wrath, therefore, describes God's permanent opposition to sin, an opposition which has been and is still being revealed in the world. In his exegesis of Romans 1:18, Professor Tasker rightly contends that this revelation of divine wrath is not a 'prophetic present' (that is, a wrath which 'is going to be revealed' in the final day of wrath, as in Romans 2:5); nor is it a 'strict present' (namely, a wrath which 'is at this moment being revealed' – its manifestation thus being restricted to Paul's day); but rather, argues Tasker, it is a 'frequentative present', that is, a wrath which 'is continually being revealed'.[3]

Manifestations of God's wrath

Both the Bible and history confirm the correctness of this exegesis. For example, the disharmony within nature and the existence of pain and death are eloquent testimonies to the divine wrath, as were the Flood and the destruction of Sodom and Gomorrah. When Israel disobeyed God, whether, for example, in the wilderness or in the period of the Judges or prior to the Exile, God's wrath was regularly stirred into activity against their sin. The destruction of both the Temple and Jerusalem in AD 70, involving the massacre of over a million Jews and the dispersing of others, must be similarly explained by the wrath of God. 'How dreadful it will be in those days for pregnant women and nursing mothers!' warns the Lord Jesus. 'There will be great distress in the land and wrath against this people' (Luke 21:23, NIV).

On the other hand, this wrath is sometimes expressed differently; such is the case in Romans 1:24,26 and 28, when God withdraws, in varying degrees, His restraints from sinners, thus allowing them uncontrolled indulgence in the most detestable and hideous forms of sin. While such indulgence is temporarily attractive, yet God's justice

3. R.V.G. Tasker, *The Biblical Doctrine of the Wrath of God* (Tyndale Press, 1951), p.9.

and wrath ensure that sinners reap what they sow. Suffering, violence, strife, anarchy, wars, immorality, crime and unhappiness follow in the wake of such sin as the manifestations of God's wrath.

Governments, magistrates, God-honouring laws, godly parents, a holy church, the knowledge of the Word, are some of the means God uses to restrain and control sin. Through such means God exercises a preventing and restraining influence upon sinners, with the result that they are often unable to indulge in the grosser sins which rage in their hearts. In this way sin is curbed and the standards of justice and morality are maintained and enjoyed within society. There are times, however, when the holy God withdraws these restraints and in His wrath abandons people to the pursuit of their evil desires. The contemporary situation in our own land needs to be understood in the light of this basic principle.

The day of wrath

The wrath of God, however, is not only manifested in the 'frequentative present', as in Romans 1:18. The Bible also teaches that this divine wrath will burst in like a flood upon the ungodly in the final 'day of wrath and revelation of the righteous judgment of God' (Rom. 2:5). It was this final manifestation of wrath to which John the Baptist referred when a group of Pharisees and Sadducees approached him one day requesting baptism. 'You brood of vipers!', he replied, 'Who warned you to flee from the coming wrath?' (Matt. 3:7, NIV). He then urged upon them the necessity of true conversion as the only means of escaping this wrath, which he symbolized in terms of 'fire' in verses 10 and 12.

Some of our Lord's parables stress this point, as, for example, in the imagery of the final 'harvest' at the end of the world; similarly the apostle Paul, speaking of his fellow-countrymen, says, 'thou . . . treasurest up unto thyself

wrath against the day of wrath' (Rom. 2:5). Whilst unbelievers are in this world 'the children of wrath' (Eph. 2:3),
and experience the wrath of God at death, there is in addition 'the day of wrath', when the divine anger will fall upon
the ungodly in a way which will be unrestrained.

In Romans 5:9 Paul again refers to this eschatological
wrath which is to be unleashed upon the unbelieving world
at the day of judgment, but here he speaks of it as a wrath
from which believers will be saved through Christ. This
point is underlined by the apostle in 1 Thessalonians 1:10,
where we read that the Lord Jesus has delivered us from
the *orgē* or 'wrath to come'. John Flavel wrote:

> He died not to precure a mitigation or abatement of the
> rigour or severity of the sentence, but to rescue his peo-
> ple fully from all degrees of wrath. So that there is no
> condemnation to them that are in Christ, Romans 8:1.
> All the wrath of God to the last drop, was squeezed out
> into that bitter cup which Christ drank of, and wrung
> out the very dregs thereof.[4]

It is in the Apocalypse, however, that the most vivid
descriptions are given of this impending wrath. In the sixth
chapter, when the sixth seal is opened, symbolizing the
introduction of the judgment day, a description is given of
the accompanying signs, such as the earthquake, the
darkness of the sun, the moon's blood-like appearance, the
rolling up of the heavens like a piece of paper, and the
moving out of position of the mountains and islands. It is
not, however, these great cataclysmic changes, nor death,
that seize the ungodly with terror, but rather the presence
of God and the 'wrath of the Lamb'. (A similar terror is
voiced in some of the Old Testament prophecies. In the
words of the prophet Zephaniah, 'The great day of the Lord
is near, it is near, and hasteth greatly, even the voice of

4.   *The Works of John Flavel* (Banner of Truth, 1968), vol. 1, p.470.

the day of the Lord: the mighty man shall cry there bitterly' (1:14). Joel adds, 'the day of the Lord is great and very terrible; and who can abide it?' (2:11), while the question posed by Malachi is, 'But who may abide the day of his coming? and who shall stand when he appeareth?' (3:2).) Here then in the Apocalypse we hear the universal cry of unbelievers: 'the great day of his wrath is come; and who shall be able to stand?' Rather than face this wrath of God, people will vainly request annihilation for themselves.

Then in Revelation 14 our attention is drawn to the victory of the church. Here a description of the bliss of the Lord's people is followed by a series of warnings to mankind of the events preceding the *parousia*, and the warning loudly issued by the third angel is that the divine wrath will fall upon all those who 'worship the beast' (vv.9,10). Here and now, of course, the wrath of God is mixed with His grace and kindness, but in the last day this wrath will be unmixed and unrelieved.

Finally, in chapter 19, after the account of the marriage of the Lamb, we are provided with a description of our victorious, conquering Saviour, here called 'Faithful and True'. He is pictured at His second appearing seated on a white horse 'smiting the nations' and 'ruling them with a rod of iron'. In other words, Christ treads 'the winepress of the fierceness and wrath of Almighty God' (v.15) by executing the divine sentence upon the ungodly.

It is within this context and against this background that we must view the ministry of the Word. The wrath of God is a fact and reality that must be preached, for it will break out upon the whole world one day, and even at death it sends the ungodly to hell.

A basic question

At this point a fundamental question must be raised as to the propriety of claiming that God reacts to sin in this way. Is not this a reaction which is unworthy of God? In a society where tolerance and permissiveness regulate the behaviour of the majority of people, the wrath of God is naturally regarded by them as an anachronism which is unintelligible and unreasonable. Here then is an objection which undermines not only the gospel, but the character of God Himself.

Dr Martyn Lloyd-Jones, commenting on Romans 3:25, argues that there is only one reason why people object to the doctrine of the wrath of God: 'It is', he claims, 'that they substitute Greek philosophy for the biblical revelation.'[5] He is correct. To the ancient Greek philosophers the concept of wrath was obnoxious; they viewed it as a mere defect of character, which needed to be eliminated from people, and even from God. They regarded God as an impassive Being who was incapable of reacting to human behaviour. Under this dominant influence, scholars and theologians throughout the present century have rejected the biblical concept of the divine wrath as something which is 'unworthy' of God and 'primitive' in origin.

In contrast, the Holy Spirit has brought us under the supreme authority of the Scriptures rather than Greek philosophy. In addition, in the case of ministers of the Word, they have been called and equipped by God to preach His infallible self-revelation.

It is at this point that ministers need to examine themselves, their beliefs and their preaching critically. Are they declaring the whole counsel of God? Does the glory of God's perfections permeate their thinking and preaching, or are they in danger of reducing God in the eyes of their congregations to a benign and helpless grandfather figure? Some may be assailed by lingering doubts concerning the divine wrath and hell, or may be reluctant to preach this doctrine for various reasons. One of the reasons is their failure to appreciate the ineffable glory of the triune God.

5. D.M. Lloyd-Jones, *Romans: An Exposition of Chapters 3.20-4.25, Atonement and Justification* (Banner of Truth, 1970), p.79.

Consequently His holiness and wrath have not been given a proper biblical emphasis and balance in their preaching.

Two contributory factors must be considered here. One is a wrong pietistic emphasis, which seeks in the main a devotional blessing or uplift, and which then shrinks from grappling with the revelation of the glory of God. This is not to depreciate the experimental, but a proper experimental approach must be God-centred, and generally speaking, we are not digging into the riches of the Word in order to gaze with awe and wonder on the glories of God. There is another factor too, and that is our difficulty in recognizing the awfulness of sin. If our view of sin is superficial and tolerant, then we are more liable to think at times that God's opposition to sin is rather extreme, with the result that we tone down (subconsciously at least) the biblical emphasis. Writing in 1700, the Rev. John Morgan, Vicar of Aberconwy, declared: 'Let not the one who understands the perfection of God marvel that the sinner deserves eternal punishment.'[6]

To underline this important point, we need to relate the perfection of God's moral nature to sin in the context of Isaiah 6, for unless we see this important relationship, our understanding of God's wrath will be defective. There are two main points to establish in this context.

1. The majesty of God

First of all, let us consider sin as an affront to the *majesty* of God. Our forefathers viewed sin in this way primarily, as an offence and insult against the infinite dignity and majesty of God.

Consider how this majesty is described in the opening words of Isaiah 6. He is, for example, 'the Lord'. The Hebrew word is *adonai*, which means He is the One who is able to carry out all His purposes. There is no weakness or failure in God at all. God is the Almighty One who

6.   University College of North Wales Library, Bangor MS.421, p.302.

declares, 'My counsel shall stand, and I will do all my pleasure' (Isa. 46:10). He is also described as 'sitting upon a throne', and here we are introduced to His sovereign rule over heaven and earth. We are then told that He is 'high and lifted up', that is, He is apart from us and wholly other than ourselves, transcendent and exalted above all. Such is the infinite majesty of God that He is surrounded by seraphs who cry out incessantly before Him the chorus 'Holy, holy, holy, is the Lord of hosts . . .' (Isa. 6:3). If you view sin in this context, you will not marvel that God is angry with the sinner and that He determines to punish him in hell.

Sin is an offence and insult against this glorious Person. 'When they knew God,' writes Paul, 'they glorified him not as God, neither were thankful; but . . . changed the glory of the incorruptible God' (Rom. 1:21,23). Sin involves a despising of the divine majesty and greatness; it is an offence against an infinite Being. As dreadful as hell is, affirms Jonathan Edwards, it is 'not more so than the Being is great and glorious against whom you have sinned . . . The wrath of God that you have heard of . . . is not more dreadful than that Majesty which you have despised and trampled on is awful.'[7]

It is in relation to God that sin assumes its essential significance: it is not a mere defect or weakness in man, or an unsociable action, but rather an offence against God. 'Against thee, thee only, have I sinned, and done this evil in thy sight,' confessed David (Ps. 51:4). 'How then can I do this great wickedness,' exclaims Joseph to Potiphar's wife, 'and sin against God?' (Gen. 39:9). Sin is active rebellion against God, opposition to His authority, contempt of His person, the breaking of His law and the despising of His Word and love.

We see this illustrated in the sin of our first parents,

---

7. *The Works of Jonathan Edwards* (Banner of Truth, 1974), vol. 2, p.887.

when they refused to submit to and obey the revealed will of God. In the words of the Puritan Samuel Bolton, 'Sin is the practical-blasphemy of all the name of God. It is the dare of His justice, the rape of His mercy, the jeer of His patience, the slight of His power, the contempt of His love.' Sin, says Ralph Venning, is 'an anti-will to God's will', or in the words of Thomas Manton, 'an affront to God's authority', 'contempt of God Himself' and 'unsubjection to God'. It is 'downright opposition to God and His Law', adds John Owen, in which 'the whole authority of God, and therein God Himself, is despised'.[8] God has created all things for His pleasure and glory; yet man has defied his Creator, and even attempts to remove God from His throne.

We must warn sinners of the One against whom they sin – that they are sinning against the all-perfect, wise, almighty, holy, infinite, loving God, who has given us all things richly to enjoy. Here is the evil of sin: it is committed against this great God, who will nevertheless ensure that His holy name will be glorified in creation, whether in the salvation of the elect or the damnation of the ungodly.

2. The holiness of God

Let us consider sin, secondly, in relation to the *holiness* of God. As the seraphs gazed upon the holy nature of God they chanted the anthem of Isaiah 6:3. Two aspects of God's holiness must be noted.

First of all, the holiness of God means that He is free from all sin. It is difficult for us to appreciate this truth, for we are ourselves so accustomed to sin. Sin is active within our lives as believers, and it is acted before our eyes in the world and, regrettably, in the church too. We live in a world dominated and permeated by sin, so it is far from easy for us to conceive of God as being free of all sin. Yet this is the testimony of the Bible: 'God is light, and in him

---

8. These definitions are quoted in E.F. Kevan, *The Grace of Law* (Carey Kingsgate Press, 1964), p.49.

is no darkness at all' (1 John 1:5). There is no trace of evil or imperfection in God; His nature shines with a purity that compels the seraphs to veil their faces in reverence.

Secondly, the holiness of God means that He hates sin with an intense hatred. Any deviation from His pure and spotless nature, and from the law which mirrors that holiness, is abhorrent to Him. Let me illustrate this point, for it is foundational to our appreciation of the divine wrath.

As a consequence of regeneration and the continuous work of the Holy Spirit in sanctification, believers have themselves a hatred of sin which is universal. I recall dealing with a particularly sordid problem on one occasion, and being compelled to leave the room with a feeling of deep abhorrence. One felt angry and sickened at what one heard. Or consider the reaction of the apostle Paul when he saw the city of Athens wholly given over to idolatry. Luke records that 'his spirit was stirred in him' (Acts 17:16); that is, Paul was angry, and there was a fire of indignation and detestation burning within him.

We must, however, multiply this kind of reaction millions and millions of times over before we begin to approximate to God's intense and perfect hatred of sin. 'For thou art not a God that hath pleasure in wickedness,' writes the psalmist, 'neither shall evil dwell with thee. The foolish shall not stand in thy sight: thou hatest all workers of iniquity ... the Lord will abhor the bloody and deceitful man' (Ps. 5:4-6). The holiness that even the angels possess is by comparison like the feeble light of a matchstick on a dark country road compared with the blaze and light of the sun at midday. Such is the contrast, and if he is to preach God's wrath with conviction and urgency, there is need for the preacher to be gripped and moved by this aspect of the divine glory.

It is because God hates sin that His wrath is stirred against the sinner, but 'it is our insensitivity to sin', writes

Jonathan Edwards, 'that prevents our realizing how hell-deserving sin is; our devilish dispositions make sin not appear "horrid"'.[9] Is this not true? Audacious, proud sinners ridicule the concept of divine wrath; even some 'evangelicals' titter in incredulity at the mention of hell; but these people do not reckon with the holiness of God. 'Hell', remarked one preacher, 'is scorched through and through by the holiness of God.' Therefore 'to sin', wrote Isaac Watts, 'is not a light and trifling matter'.

How hateful is sin to us? Are the truths of the wrath and holiness of God, for us, only theories which leave us soundly unmoved? One thing is certain. If we fail to reckon with the infinite holiness of God, the wrath of God will always remain for us a difficult doctrine. God hates all sin, including the sins committed by Christians. His holy nature cannot compromise with sin or tolerate it anywhere; not even on the cross did the holy God change His attitude towards sin, but He punished it in the Person of our Redeemer, thus magnifying His justice and holiness. One of the reasons why Martin Luther distinguished between the merciful wrath of God and the wrath of His severity was because of God's universal hatred of sin. The merciful wrath of God is shown to the saints, leading them to repentance and faith. While God chastises and humbles believers for their sin, His wrath towards them remains a merciful wrath; but the wrath of His severity He reserves for the ungodly, and it always leads to hell.

Evangelism

Before we conclude this brief study of the divine wrath, we need to relate this doctrine to evangelism, and more especially to the work of the preacher of the gospel.

In 2 Peter 3 the apostle gives us a twofold reason why the day of the Lord has not yet come. The first reason

9. John Gerstner, *Jonathan Edwards on Heaven and Hell* (Baker, 1980), p.81.

concerns the character of God, namely, His eternity and faithfulness (vv.8,9). The second reason, which we must emphasize, has to do with the purpose of God, and in this context there are three points which can be underlined and applied.

First, Peter tells us that God is 'longsuffering' towards us. While God's wrath is a fact, yet He is extremely patient and forbearing with sinners. The way in which John Elias disciplined his children is an instructive example of long-suffering. He firmly believed in correcting and punishing his children, but on the first offence he would only rebuke the child. If the offence was repeated, Elias would issue a further rebuke, but this time, in addition, he would extract a promise that the child would not misbehave again. When the bad behaviour was repeated a third time, John Elias used a rod to punish the child, but first of all he prayed with his wife, beseeching God's mercy for their child.[10] Elias was certainly not guilty of impetuous or bad-tempered behaviour towards his children; his response to their sin was a controlled and patient one.

Now Peter is saying something similar in this verse. The wrath of God is the controlled reaction of God's holy nature to sin, but it is a wrath He holds back for as long as possible. He will justly punish sinners, but He stays His hand of wrath for as long as possible, as He did in the days of Noah and prior to the Exile. The reason, then, why this awful day of wrath has not yet arrived is owing to God's kindness and longsuffering towards us.

When faced with suffering and the desperate needs of other people, even Christians can be indifferent and heart-less in their response. We know, for example, that unbe-lievers are in the greatest danger, yet our attempts to reach them with the gospel are pathetic and half-hearted. Our Lord wept over Jerusalem, but it is a rare occurrence

10. A most helpful biography which this writer commends is *John Elias, Life and Letters* by Edward Morgan (Banner of Truth, 1973).

today for His people to weep in prayer for the vast multitudes of people who are speeding towards hell. Are we projecting our own heartlessness and indifference on to God? If so, we are misrepresenting Him, for He burns in love and passionate concern for sinners. Peter continues by saying He is 'not willing that any should perish'. God is not a heartless being. 'As I live, saith the Lord God, I have no pleasure in the death of the wicked' (Ezek. 33:11). Hell is a dreadful punishment, but God does not gloat over the prospect of hell or the punishment of sinners in hell.

The final statement to be noted here is 'but that all should come to repentance'. Although God's purpose is the saving of His elect, His goodness and love invite and command all to repentance. Yet, according to verse 10, the doors will be closed one day, the end will come, and the day of grace will pass away. We find ourselves today in a day of grace and opportunity. The great day of the Lord's wrath has not yet come. So, while there is still time, we must declare to sinners the glorious gospel of Christ.

6
Final Judgment

In much the same way as the divine wrath culminates in the great day of wrath, so the judgment of God upon sinners reaches its climax in the final judgment. 'The Lord is a God of judgment,' says Isaiah (30:18), and He is so continually, both in the affairs of this life and more personally at death, when our destinies are sealed in private and personal judgment (Heb. 9:27). Nevertheless, the Scriptures also look forward to a final judgment, which is associated in the Old Testament with 'the day of the Lord' (Amos 5:18ff.; Zeph. 1:14ff.; Mal. 4:1, etc.), and in the New Testament with the personal return of the Lord Jesus in glory (e.g. Matt. 25:31-46).

Dispensationalists and pre-millennialists believe that there are at least three different final judgments. First of all, they distinguish a judgment of risen and living believers, which will take place immediately at the second coming of Christ. The purpose of this judgment will be to distribute rewards and vindicate the Lord's people. Then, they teach, some seven years later, at the day or revelation of Christ immediately following the great tribulation, there will be another judgment in which the Gentile nations will be judged as nations. Thirdly, a thousand years later, they claim, will follow the judgment of the unbelieving dead, which will take place before the great white throne.

Others believe, however, that the Scriptures speak not of several judgments, but of one judgment at the end of the world. For example, the Lord warns, 'Many will say to me in that day . . .' (Matt. 7:22); further, the apostle Paul declares, 'he hath appointed a day, in the which he will judge the world in righteousness by that man whom he hath ordained' (Acts 17:31); Peter, too, speaks of the heavens and the earth being 'reserved unto fire against the day of judgment and perdition of ungodly men' (2 Pet. 3:7). Without pursuing the argument we must underline basic principles relating to the final judgment which are relevant to the theme of God's wrath and also to the preaching of the gospel.

There are four aspects of the final judgment which we need briefly to emphasize:

1. Its inseparable relationship to the wrath of God

Rather than being a change of subject, final judgment is necessarily related to the character and glory of God. We can observe this in several ways.

In the first place, the law by which God will judge people is not an arbitrary standard, but the expression of His holy nature and will. It is the One who is *holy,* declares Peter, who 'judgeth according to every man's work' (1 Pet. 1:17).

Again, God's *justice* is inseparably related to this final day of judgment. The justice of God is the attribute by which He deals in vengeance with all the violations of His law, and in the final judgment He will dispense rewards and punishments both to humans and angels. All the injustices, wickedness, hypocrisy and irregularities that mar the life of the world will be punished then, and this retributive justice will be a signal expression of the wrath of God. In this world it often seems as if corruption and might prevail rather than justice, and sometimes there seems to be no God in heaven. But although God allows injustice to continue here, He records human deeds in His book, and He has appointed Christ to judge the world and execute a righteous judgment.

Furthermore, as God's supreme purpose in the world is His own glory, the final judgment will provide a glorious display of His *majesty and authority*. This will be a public judgment, as distinct from a private one as at death; it will involve the judgment of body and soul and will be confirmatory in character. This public, universal judgment will be the platform on which God will display to the whole world His glorious Person, including His fierce wrath, His strict justice and His amazing love. We must view the final judgment, then, as a necessary and glorious expression and vindication of the justice and wrath of God.

2. Christ Himself the Judge

In His mediatorial role Christ will be the Judge. As He Himself tells us, God the Father 'hath given him authority to execute judgment also, because he is the Son of man' (John 5:27). The privilege, then, of judging men and angels has been granted to Christ as part of His reward and exaltation for His obedience 'unto death, even the death of the cross' (Phil. 2:8). 'Judgment', explains John Flavel, 'is the act of the whole undivided Trinity. The Father and Spirit judge, as well as Christ, in respect of authority and consent, but it is the act of Christ, in respect of visible management and execution.'[1] Thus, since the Father and the Holy Spirit judge by Him, the Lord can say without contradiction, 'the Father judgeth no man, but hath committed all judgment unto the Son' (John 5:22).

The act of judging relates, of course, to the kingly office of the Lord Jesus. Because of His humiliation He did not regularly exercise this kingly office when He was upon earth, though we see examples of His kingship in His triumphant entry into Jerusalem prior to His death, and also in the title Pilate wrote over His cross – 'This is Jesus the King of the Jews'. In the final judgment, however, this kingly office of the Saviour will be apparent for all to see.

Jonathan Edwards, in his usually thorough way,

1. *The Works of John Flavel* (Banner of Truth, 1968), vol.1, p.525.

suggests six reasons for the appropriateness of Christ being appointed judge of the world rather than the Father:

1.   God seeth fit, that he who is in the **human nature,** should be the judge of those who are of the human nature.

2.   Christ hath this honour . . . given him, as a **suitable reward** for his sufferings.

3.   It is needful that Christ should be the judge of the world, in order that he may **finish** the work of redemption . . . Now, the redemption of fallen man . . . is actually fulfilled, in converting sinners . . . in carrying them on in the way of grace . . . and in finally raising their bodies to life, in glorifying them, in pronouncing the blessed sentence upon them, in crowning them with honour and glory in the sight of men and angels, and in completing and perfecting their reward.

4.   It was proper that he who is appointed king of the church should rule till he should have put all his enemies under his feet; in order to which, he must be the judge of his **enemies,** as well as of his people . . . and then he will deliver up the kingdom to the Father: 1 Cor. 15:24,25 . . . it is proper that he who at present reigns, and is carrying on the war against those who are of the opposite kingdom, should have the honour of obtaining the victory, and finishing the war.

5.   It is for the abundant **comfort of the saints** that Christ is appointed to be their judge . . . the same person who spilled his blood for them hath the determination of their state left with him . . . What matter of joy to them will it be at the last day, to lift up their eyes, and behold the person in whom they have trusted for salvation . . . and whose voice they have often heard inviting them to himself for protection and safety, coming to judge them.

6.   That Christ is appointed to be the judge of the world, will be for the more abundant **conviction of the ungodly** . . . How justly will they be condemned by him whose salvation they have rejected . . . and whom they have pierced by their sins! [2]

We must proclaim, as did the apostle, that the One who died for sinners is the King who will return gloriously to earth one day and judge all men: 'God . . . hath appointed a day, in the which he will judge the world in righteousness by that man whom he hath ordained' (Acts 17:30,31). God does not merely invite or beseech sinners, but He also commands them to repent. On the authority of God's Word we too must command sinners in this authoritative way.

3. The majesty of the Judge

'If Felix trembled when Paul preached of judgment (Acts 24:25)', exclaims Thomas Watson, 'how will sinners tremble when they shall see Christ come to judgment!' [3] Certainly the majesty of the scene will be breath-taking, especially when the Judge Himself appears in His unveiled glory to judge mankind.

The brief glimpses we have in the New Testament of Christ's glory during His earthly ministry help us to appreciate something of the majesty of His appearance at the final judgment. Matthew, in his account of the transfiguration, tells us that the Lord Jesus was '*transfigured*', that is, 'transformed' (Matt. 17:2). Luke uses a different word, saying that 'the fashion of his countenance was *altered*', that is, while His face remained the same, its *appearance* was transformed (Luke 9:29). According to Matthew, 'his face did shine as the sun' – 'with an innate, inherent light', suggests Matthew Henry, 'the more sensibly glorious, because it suddenly broke out, as it were,

2.   *The Works of Jonathan Edwards*, vol.2, pp.193-4.
3.   Thomas Watson, A *Body of Divinity* (Banner of Truth, 1958), p.218.

from behind a dark cloud'. [4] His clothes, too, were 'white as the light'. The explanation for this, of course, is that His whole body was altered just as His face was, and the light of His glory shone through His clothes. So Luke could describe them as 'glistening', for He was one blaze of celestial glory.

On the last day, however, what the world will see will be Christ's Person in unveiled and magnificent glory, and this will be an awe-inspiring sight. Let us consider briefly three descriptions of this scene in the New Testament. The first is our Lord's own description: He pictures the Son of Man accompanied by the angels and seated 'upon the throne of his glory' – a throne of unimaginable splendour, matching the splendour of its occupant (Matt. 25:31). Secondly, in 2 Thessalonians 1:7 we find the apostle Paul using the Greek word *apokalupsis* to describe the descent of Christ from heaven: the Lord in His glory will then be fully 'disclosed' and 'uncovered' for the entire world to see. At the same time, the accompanying angels will be surrounded by fire, indicating the holiness of God manifest in judgment. The final picture is John's vision of 'a great white throne, and him that sat on it' (Rev. 20:11). The appearance of Christ upon this throne is so terrifying that earth and heaven run away from Him in fear. Jesus Christ will then be clearly revealed as the Judge, and all creatures will be compelled to acknowledge His deity and glory.

4. The basis of judgment

While angels will assist Christ in judgment (Matt. 13: 41,42; 25:31), it is clear that the fallen angels will be judged themselves (Matt. 8:29; 1 Cor. 6:3; 2 Pet. 2:4; Jude 6), as well as every human person, whether alive or dead (Eccl. 12:14; Matt. 25:32; 2 Cor. 5:10; Rev. 20:12).

4. *Matthew Henry's Commentary* (Marshall, Morgan & Scott, 1953), vol.5, p.242.

Judgment of believers

Believers themselves will be judged in the last day, although, of course, they will not be liable for *condemnatory* judgment, for they have been justified through Christ and eternally saved from the wrath to come. In considering the significance of this judgment for the elect we can appeal to several verses.

The words found in 2 Corinthians 5:10 are pertinent and extremely challenging, showing that there can be no question but that all believers will be judged: 'For we must all appear before the judgment seat of Christ; that every one may receive the things done in his body, according to that he hath done, whether it be good or bad.'

Several words in this verse deserve comment. Bengel reminds us that the word 'appear' means that 'we must all stand revealed in our true character before the judgment seat of Christ'. There will be no possibility of pretence or deception before the omniscient Judge. We shall be laid bare before Him, 'stripped of every outward façade of respectability', writes P.E. Hughes, 'and openly revealed in the full and true reality of one's character. All our hypocrisies and concealments, all our secret, intimate sins of thought and deed, will be opened to the scrutiny of Christ'.[5]

The thought of 'the judgment seat of Christ' should not depress us, but rather serve as a stimulus to greater zeal and obedience. 'Let us then imagine Christ's judgment seat to be present now,' pleads Chrysostom, 'and reckon each one of us with his own conscience, and account the Judge to be already present and everything to be revealed and brought forth. For we must not merely stand but also be manifested. Do you not blush?' A similar thought is found in 1 Corinthians 3:13 – 'Every man's work shall be made

---

5. P.E. Hughes, *Paul's Second Epistle to the Corinthians* (Marshall, Morgan & Scott, 1962), p.180.

manifest: for the day shall declare it, because it shall be revealed by fire'. Believers, and especially preachers, will undergo a searching test, for the day will 'declare' or 'show' in its true character the quality rather than the quantity of our work.

What is the purpose of this judgment for believers? According to 1 Corinthians 3:14, 'he shall receive a reward' (or 'wage'). This is not a reference to salvation, but to a reward within salvation for the quality of our work. We see from 2 Corinthians 5:10 that the purpose is not wholly negative, for it includes the disclosure and reward of what is both good and bad. Dr Philip Hughes warns us against viewing this judgment as the reflecting of punishment upon believers: 'The judgment pronounced is not a declaration of doom but an assessment of worth with the assignment of rewards',[6] but all within the framework of grace and salvation. The rewards will vary from one believer to another according to the degree of faithfulness and diligence shown (Luke 19:16ff.).

One question which especially troubles believers when they hear mention of this judgment is, If God has forgiven us, how can He recall our sins again? Some contend that our sins will not be raised in the day of judgment. The implication of Scripture, however, is that our sins will be 'manifest', but only as forgiven sins. The fact that God will judge 'every idle word' (Matt. 12:36) and 'the secrets of men' (Rom. 2:16), as well as 'according to that he hath done' (2 Cor. 5:10), suggests that our sins will not be excluded, for all will be 'manifest'. How then does this square with forgiveness? It must be that while we shall see our sin, we shall see it only in the light of His covenant of grace; and seeing it as sin washed in the blood of Christ, we shall then be the more able to admire and praise the riches of God's grace in Christ.

6. ibid., p.180.

Here there are two points of application to be made. First of all, this fact of judgment should make us more zealous and faithful in our service of the Lord Jesus. After mentioning the fact and significance of the judgment seat of Christ, the apostle goes on immediately to say, 'Knowing therefore the terror of the Lord, we persuade men' (2 Cor. 5:11). These words are very significant. The apostle is filled with awe at the thought of his Lord and the prospect of judgment, and in the light of this he is more constrained to 'persuade men', both believers and unbelievers. Does the judgment seat of Christ have this effect upon your life and ministry?

Secondly, it is helpful to note how the apostle applies this principle of judgment in 1 Corinthians 4:1-5, by urging ministers to be faithful stewards, irrespective of the opinion and attitude of people towards them. The only competent judge is the Lord, so we must wait for His appearance, when judgment will be meted out to all, including believers. 'The Lord . . . will bring to light the hidden things of darkness' – whether motives, actions or thoughts – 'and will make manifest the counsels of the hearts.' Here is infallible and perfect judgment: 'and then' – and only then – 'shall every man have praise of God'. Ministers must not be preoccupied with and distressed by the unfair and ungodly behaviour of people who oppose them; instead they must maintain their integrity, follow after holiness, continue in faithful service of the Lord, and keep their eyes on the future, for the Lord will one day deal with all people, including themselves.

Judgment of unbelievers

With respect to the judgment of unbelievers, the basis will be the revealed will of God, both for those who are ignorant of the gospel and for those who have been privileged to hear the gospel.

Some Christians believe that only those who have rejected the gospel will be judged. One implication of this view is that pagans who have never heard of the way of salvation will be spared from appearing before the Judge or, if they do appear, will get off comparatively lightly. It is surprising how popular and widespread this belief is. Christians who hold it are suggesting that there is a double standard, depending on whether or not people have heard the gospel; this means that in the final judgment the pagan will be better off for not having heard the gospel.

This popular belief is, however, unbiblical. People are guilty and condemned, whether they have heard the gospel or not. Paul states, 'by one man sin entered into the world, and death by sin; and so death passed upon *all* men, for that all have sinned . . . by the offence of one judgment came upon all men to condemnation' (Rom. 5:12,18). The argument, therefore, that unbelief is the only sin meriting judgment and condemnation is an unbiblical one. Unbelief is, of course, a great sin, so that the person who does not believe is condemned; but unbelief is not the only reason for condemnation. Before a missionary pioneers the gospel in a pagan area, and before a minister preaches to people in his vicinity, those people are already guilty and under the wrath of God.

An important question, and one to which we need to be sensitive at this point, is this: *Is it fair for God to judge the heathen who have not heard the gospel at all?* The biblical answer includes the following important principles.

First of all, *God's judgment is always just and right.* 'We are sure', says Paul, 'that the judgment of God is according to truth' (Rom. 2:2); again, in the words of the apostle John, 'in righteousness he doth judge' (Rev. 19:11), and according to the psalmist, 'he shall judge the world in righteousness, he shall minister judgment to the people in uprightness' (Ps. 9:8). The testimony of the Bible is that God is never unfair or biased in His judgment. We must guard this principle jealously, as it concerns the glory of God's character.

In the second place, passages like Matthew 11:21-24 and Romans 2:12-16 teach us that *there are degrees of knowledge and of sin and, consequently, degrees of rewards and punishments.* 'The longer sinners live,' argues Jonathan Edwards, 'the more wrath they accumulate.' This is one reason why Edwards pleaded with children not to start living a life of sin but to be converted at an early age. 'All men', he adds, 'partake equally of original sin, but men do not partake equally of "actual sins", so that the sooner the persevering sinner dies the better!'[7] Some people, our Lord says, are more privileged than others, and more responsible. For this reason it will be more tolerable in the day of judgment for pagan cities like Tyre, Sidon, Sodom and Gomorrah than for Bethsaida and Capernaum. All these cities will be judged and punished, for no one is let off lightly; yet there will be greater punishment for some than for others.

Finally, an examination of what Paul says in Romans 2 helps us to see more clearly the basis of God's judgment. He first states the basic principle, namely, that He 'will render to every man according to his deeds' (v.6), and then proceeds to expand it in the verses that follow. Continuing in verses 11-16, he teaches that *the important question is not knowledge or ignorance, but sin.* All who sin, whether in ignorance or in knowledge of the law, are regarded by God as transgressors, and they will therefore be rewarded according to their deeds.

But is this fair to the unenlightened and pagan Gentiles? The answer of Paul is in verses 14 and 15. The Gentiles who are without the written Law nevertheless have law written on their hearts, so they have an innate moral consciousness. Hendriksen suggests we should accordingly

7. Gerstner, *Jonathan Edwards on Heaven and Hell*, p.65.

preface verse 16 with the words 'All this will become clear'[8] – that is, thoughts, words, motives and actions will be exposed and judged in that day.

Implications

Now this is an important point in relation to our preaching today. It is not enough for us to give textual exegesis and preach soundly; in addition, we must use what Spurgeon called 'heart argument'. The truth must be addressed to the minds in the first place, but preachers dare not stop there; the consciences of the hearers must also be touched and stirred by the application of the law of God. It is a fact of the utmost significance that humans are all created in the image of God and have 'the work of the law' written upon their consciences, thus providing what Cornelius Van Til has described as 'the point of contact'.[9] 'Deep down in his mind', writes Van Til, 'every man knows that he is the creature of God and responsible to God. Every man, at bottom, knows that he is a covenant-breaker. But every man acts and talks as though this were not so. It is the one point that cannot bear mentioning in his presence.'[10] For this reason, if preachers do not aim for the consciences as well as the minds of their hearers, they will be defective in their work.

The doctrine of final judgment also implies human responsibility and accountability. Men and women are held responsible by God for their own sin: 'the soul that sinneth,' God warns, 'it shall die' (Ezek. 18:4). It will not be possible to hide behind or blame other people for one's own sin. The punishment of sin will be borne by those who commit sin, unless, of course, they become Christians. Here is a truth which must be emphasized in evangelistic

8. William Hendriksen, *Romans 1-8* (Banner of Truth, 1981), p.97.
9. Cornelius Van Til, *Apologetics* (1966), ch.3: 'The Point of Contact', pp.38-58.
10. ibid., p.57.

preaching. Despite even the pervasiveness, corruption and dominance of sin throughout man's entire nature and the consequent inability to please or obey God, man is still held responsible by God for his sin and his response to the gospel.[11] Whatever his attitude to God and sin may be, the sinner must be informed of this basic and alarming truth.

There is another sobering aspect to the subject of human responsibility, namely, the responsibility and accountability of preachers and elders to God for the quality and extent of their work. This note is sounded repeatedly throughout the Bible. The prophet Ezekiel, for example, is told, 'I have made thee a watchman unto the house of Israel: therefore hear the word at my mouth, and give them warning from me' (Ezek. 3:17). God then warns His servant:

> When I say unto the wicked, Thou shalt surely die; and thou givest him not warning, nor speakest to warn the wicked from his wicked way, to save his life; the same wicked man shall die in his iniquity; but his blood will I require at thine hand. Yet if thou warn the wicked, and he turn not from his wickedness, nor from his wicked way, he shall die in his iniquity; but thou hast delivered thy soul. (Ezek. 3:18,19)

On this passage Patrick Fairbairn comments:

> A salutary lesson is conveyed here to all who are put in trust with souls, as well in regard to the nature of the charge itself, as to the manner in which it ought to be fulfilled. It is emphatically the work of God they have to do, and the instrument to be wielded in the doing of it is his own word. Let this be plied with unwearied diligence, with affectionate tenderness and fervency of spirit; for the work is of infinite importance, and results past reckoning depend on it. Eternal weal or woe grows

11. There are two helpful footnotes on this subject in A.W. Pink's *The Sovereignty of God* (Banner of Truth, 1961), pp.99,108.

out of it to all who come within the field of its oper-
ations. And for oneself – whatever may be the result for
others – the path of duty is the only path of safety;
faithfulness to God must be the supreme rule, and his
glory the chief aim. 'I have a commission to fulfil, I must
deliver my own soul,' – let this be the one answer to all
counter – solicitations from the flesh or the world; and
it will also be the best guarantee of ultimate success.[12]

In all probability the apostle Paul had these words from
Ezekiel in mind when he declared to the Ephesian elders
at Miletus, 'Wherefore I take you to record this day, that I
am pure from the blood of all men' (Acts 20:26). This claim
was made only after three years of intensive and zealous
evangelism in Ephesus, during which all the inhabitants
had heard the gospel through Paul, either publicly or in
their homes (v.20). Such care for souls on the apostle's
part absolved him from blame and responsibility in the day
of judgment.

A similar principle is found in Hebrews 13:17, where
submission to church officers is adjoined. It is clear here
that elders and preachers carry a heavy and solemn
responsibility, for 'they watch for your souls, as they that
must give account'. Such is their responsibility that David
Dickson described the ministry as 'the most dangerous of
all charges, because the account of lost souls within the
church shall be craved at their hands, whether they have
done all that which became them to do'.[13]

The Scottish preacher, John Welch, felt this sense of
responsiblity greatly and spent at least eight to ten hours
daily in prayer. Even in the middle of the night he would
frequently rise to pray for his people. His wife naturally
expressed concern at seeing him out of bed on a cold winter

12. Patrick Fairbairn, *An Exposition of Ezekiel* (Grand Rapids: Sovereign
    Grace Publishers, 1971), p.23.
13. James Ferguson and David Dickson, *The Epistles of Paul and
    Hebrews* (Banner of Truth, 1978), 'Hebrews', p.80.

evening with only a plaid wrapped around him while he prayed. Welch's answer was: 'O woman, I have the souls of three thousand to answer for, and I know not how it is with many of them.' In the light of the fast approaching day of judgment, we all need to show the same diligence and burden for souls.

7
Hell
Some Definitions

As there are four words which are translated 'hell' in the Authorized Version of the Bible, we must begin by carefully defining these words. This is especially important because liberal scholars, as well as the proponents of conditional immortality who espouse annihilation, claim that our belief in a traditional hell is owing to ignorance and prejudice. For example, Seventh Day Adventists, Christadelphians and Jehovah's Witnesses insist that we have misunderstood the correct significance of these biblical words. This is a serious charge, and one which we need to answer immediately.

The four words translated 'hell' in the Authorized Version are She'ol, Hades, Tartarus and Gehenna. We shall examine each in turn.

Tartarus

This is a Greek name for the underworld, and especially for the abode of the damned. It is used only once in the New Testament, in a verbal form ('cast down to Tartarus') in 2 Peter 2:4. Here Peter is describing the punishment of God upon the fallen angels; they are consigned to a place of intense darkness which functions as a prison for its inhabitants. Clearly therefore this is a reference to hell.

The real controversy, however, rages around the other three words, which we must now consider in more detail.

She'ol and Hades

One of the most common Hebrew words to describe the location of the dead is *she'ol*, which means 'the depths' or 'the unseen state'. This word occurs 65 times in the Old

Testament. Another word similar to it is the Greek word *hades*, which appears ten times in the New Testament. What then is the significance of these two words? If we study their usage in the Old and New Testaments we will find that they are employed in more than one sense. This fact is crucial to a correct understanding of them.

Sometimes the word *she'ol* denotes the state of death into which believers and unbelievers alike are brought; references like 1 Samuel 2:6, Job 14:13,14 and 17:13,14, and Psalm 89:48, all have this connotation. Similarly in the New Testament the term *hades* sometimes has this meaning. In Acts 2:27 and Revelation 6:8 this is clearly the case: what is signified in these passages is not 'hell' as such, but the state of being physically dead.

At other times, however, the word *she'ol* can have the more restricted meaning of 'the grave', as in Job 7:9 and Genesis 37:35. One Watch Tower article ridicules the doctrine of eternal hell by suggesting that, according to this latter verse, when Jacob died he went bodily into hell (*she'ol*).[1] This is a biased judgment, however, for in this and a few other contexts in Scripture the word *she'ol* simply means 'the grave'.

But, thirdly, it must be said emphatically that these words are also used in passages where 'hell' is clearly in view. For example, in Psalm 9:17 God warns the ungodly of their future punishment, and in Deuteronomy 32:22 we are told that the wrath of God burns in *she'ol*. Likewise, in at least six out of the ten New Testament references, *hades* is used in this sense, the most obvious example being Luke 16:23, where Dives is described as being 'in hell . . . in torments'.

One argument used by conditionalists against the orthodox doctrine of hell is that the word used by the Lord Jesus here is *hades*, and not *gehenna*, and that according to Revelation 20:14 even *hades* is to be cast one day into

1. Quoted in E.C. Gruss, *Apostles of Denial* (Baker, 1974), p.163.

the lake of fire. So, they claim, the passage is pictorial rather than literal. Two comments must suffice here, for the teaching of annihilation will be considered at a later stage. In the first place, our Lord's use of the word *hades* rather than *gehenna* in Luke 16:23 does not constitute an argument against eternal punishment, for the former term is more frequently used to denote hell than to denote the state of death. Secondly, what the word *hades* signifies in Revelation 20:14 is the state of death which results from the cessation of physical life.

The Lord Jesus in His human nature was in *hades*, that is, in a state of physical death, whereas His *gehenna* was experienced on the cross, where He drank to the full the cup of the Father's wrath against sinners. Peter reminds us in Acts 2 that it was impossible for *hades* to hold the Son of God indefinitely. Christ rose from the dead, and now, according to Revelation 1:18, He has the 'the keys of death and Hades'. With reference to this statement Hendriksen asks, 'Does not the Son of Man reveal that He has the keys of death whenever He welcomes the soul of a believer into heaven? And does He not prove that He has the keys of Hades when at His second coming He reunites the soul and body of the believer, a body now gloriously transformed?'[2]

With respect to Revelation 20:14, the context is that of judgment and the general resurrection of the dead which will take place at the last day. The sea is pictured as giving up all its dead; so also do death (the separation of soul and body) and Hades (the state of separation). In this sense both death and Hades cease at the last day, for never again, either in heaven or in hell, will there be a separation between body and soul. Thus, in graphic, pictorial language, death and Hades are described as being cast into the lake of fire.

Louis Berkhof, who provides us with a brief but helpful

2. William Hendriksen, *More Than Conquerors* (Tyndale Press, 1966), p.57.

survey of the meaning and use of the words *she'ol* and *hades* in the Scriptures, concludes his study in this way: 'In the Old Testament the word *sheol* is used more often for grave and less often for hell, while in the corresponding use of *hades* in the New Testament the contrary holds.'[3] This conclusion is a fair and responsible one, allowing for the varied use of these two words in the Bible. William Hendriksen sheds further light on our understanding of *hades.* He argues that when the word is used in relation to the intermediate state, it refers to 'the abode of the *souls* of the wicked *before* the judgment day'; whereas when the word *gehenna* is used, 'the reference is *generally* to the abode of the wicked, *body and soul, after* the judgment day'.[4]

Gehenna

Gehenna was the name of a valley south-west of Jerusalem where children had once been sacrificed by fire to a pagan idol named Molech. King Josiah later desecrated this pagan site, and it was then used for the burning of the city's rubbish and offal. The name was used in New Testament times as a symbol of future and eternal punishment, but several of the twelve references to Gehenna in the New Testament support Hendriksen's contention. The word is used seven times by Matthew; note especially Matthew 10:28 – 'And fear not them which kill the body, but are not able to kill the soul: but rather fear him which is able to destroy both soul and body in hell.' It is also used three times in Mark 9:43-47. These verses draw a vivid contrast between hell and life, the only alternative destinies facing mankind; our Lord warns that it is possible to go with 'two hands', 'two feet' and 'two eyes' into hell fire.

Having considered these three important words, we can say by way of summary that *she'ol* and *hades* refer to the grave as well as to the state of death, but that they also

3. Louis Berkhof, *Systematic Theology* (Banner of Truth, 1959), p.686.
4. W. Hendriksen, *The Bible on the Life Hereafter* (Baker, 1975), pp.196-7.

refer sometimes to the state of the ungodly in hell. While *she'ol* is used less frequently for hell in the New Testament, *hades* carries the meaning of hell more frequently in the New Testament, and refers to the abode and punishment of the ungodly before the general resurrection of the body. *Gehenna* describes the same place, that is, hell, but includes in it (and this is unique to the term *gehenna*) the punishment of both body and soul which will occur immediately after the final judgment.

Against this background we can appreciate the urgency and directness which characterized the proclamation of the gospel in the New Testament. Sinners are in the greatest danger, for hell awaits them unless they believe. Preaching on Matthew 8:11-12, C.H. Spurgeon quotes a minister who told his congregation, 'If you do not love the Lord Jesus Christ you will be sent to that place which it is not polite to mention.' Spurgeon gives us his opinion of this preacher:

> He ought not to have been allowed to preach again, I am sure, if he could not use plain words. Now, if I saw that house on fire over there, do you think I would stand and say, 'I believe the operation of combustion is proceeding yonder!'? No, I would call out, 'Fire! Fire!' and then everybody would know what I meant. So, if the Bible says, 'The children of the kingdom shall be cast out into outer darkness,' am I to stand here and mince the matter at all? God forbid. We must speak the truth as it is written. It is a terrible truth, for it says **'the children of the kingdom'** shall be cast out![5]

This is precisely what our Lord did. 'And fear not them which kill the body, but are not able to kill the soul,' our Saviour taught, 'but rather fear him which is able to destroy both soul and body in hell' (Matt. 10:28). Again, He

5. C.H. Spurgeon, *New Park Street Pulpit* (Banner of Truth, 1963), vol.1 (1855), p.306.

warned, 'if thy hand offend thee, cut it off: it is better for thee to enter into life maimed, than having two hands to go into hell, into the fire that never shall be quenched: where their worm dieth not, and the fire is not quenched' (Mark 9:43,44).

In some of His parables, too, such warnings are clearly expressed. The parable of the wheat and tares concludes with these words: 'The Son of man shall send forth his angels, and they shall gather out of his kingdom all things that offend, and them which do iniquity; and shall cast them into a furnace of fire: there shall be wailing and gnashing of teeth' (Matt. 13:41,42). In the parable immediately following it, our Lord warns: 'So shall it be at the end of the world: the angels shall come forth, and sever the wicked from among the just, and shall cast them into the furnace of fire' (Matt. 13:49,50).

Looking forward to the general resurrection of the dead, the Saviour revealed that 'the hour is coming, in the which all that are in the graves shall hear his voice, and shall come forth; they that have done good, unto the resurrection of life; and they that have done evil, unto the resurrection of damnation' (John 5:28,29). And in answer to people who were disturbed about certain incidents He said, 'Except ye repent, ye shall all likewise perish' (Luke 13:3-5). Later in that same Gospel He described Dives: 'he . . . being in torments . . . seeth Abraham afar off, and Lazarus in his bosom, and he cried . . . ' (Luke 16:23,24).

Notice, first, that in the majority of these references the Lord Jesus was instructing and warning His followers, informing them in detail of eternal issues such as life and death, heaven and hell and the end of the world. Whilst He did not confine His teaching to them, He did concentrate on their instruction and preparation. I wonder whether the general vagueness of belief concerning hell, and its remoteness from church life, are owing to the failure of preachers to instruct and warn believers sufficiently.

Notice, secondly, that our Lord did not shrink from emphasizing hell in His ministry; in fact, He frequently used imagery and symbolism to convey to His listeners a sense of its awfulness. What emphasis is given to hell by present-day evangelical ministers? How frequently do they preach on this subject? To refer to hell briefly or occasionally, or to talk about it in vague terms, is inadequate, for there is a wealth of biblical material on hell which must be preached if the whole counsel of God is to be declared.

Finally, notice that our Lord preached this and other doctrines authoritatively. There was nothing apologetic or diffident or uncertain in His proclamation of judgment and hell, for He knew He was referring to something true, certain and awful. Could this be said of preaching today? One verse that greatly influenced John Bunyan throughout his preaching ministry was Revelation 21:5, and especially the words, 'he that sat upon the throne said . . .' So deeply aware was he of the divine origin of his message that he preached with considerable certainty and conviction. That is a need today also. Preachers are not suggesting possibilities to people, nor are they conveying to them the fruit of their own speculation; they are proclaiming the verities which God has revealed to them in His Word.

Our Lord and the apostles, then, held out one of two possible destinies for mankind – heaven or hell, life or death. We all stand on the brink of eternity, and we will either experience salvation in heaven or suffer damnation in hell. These are the only alternatives before us, and beyond death there are no further opportunities of salvation for the unbelieving. All this adds to the seriousness and urgency of the work of preachers. They must preach as dying men to dying men, pleading with sinners to repent before it is too late.

Before proceeding to a description of hell, we must consider briefly two modifications of this biblical teaching, namely, purgatory and second probation.

Purgatory

As formulated by the Roman Catholic Church, purgatory is an abode available after death to the imperfect 'faithful' of the Roman Church; it is preparatory to heaven, and here people stay for longer or shorter periods until they purge away their sin. The ramifications of this teaching will be familiar to many: for example, prayers for the dead, indulgences, lack of assurance, and the serious undermining of the sufficiency and finality of the Saviour's sacrifice.

However, Roman Catholics, and particularly Roman Catholic charismatics with their new-found interest in the Bible, are using Scripture increasingly to support their belief in purgatory and other Popish errors. We can dismiss as irresponsible exegesis their appeal to Matthew 3:11 (particularly the words 'he shall baptize you with the Holy Ghost, and with fire'); likewise also to 1 Corinthians 3:15 ('he himself shall be saved; yet so as by fire'), and Jude 22,23 ('. . . others save with fear, pulling them out of the fire'). And though at first sight their appeal to verses in Peter's first epistle is more persuasive, upon examination it becomes clear that these verses too lend no support whatever to a belief in purgatory or the possibility of a second chance after death:

a) *1 Peter 3:18-20.* The purpose of Peter in this passage is to provide his readers with encouragement and comfort in face of persecution and to remind them of the fact of judgment and the approaching end (e.g., 1 Pet. 4:5-7). Basically, his message in verses 18-20 is that Christ has suffered and died in the flesh for our sin (v. 18). What He did in His earthly ministry (such as preaching), He now continues to do, but with this important difference: He does it now in the Spirit and through the apostles. A parallel situation was the judgment and Flood at the time of Noah; but before that judgment, too, Christ preached in the Spirit through Noah, and he and his family were saved. Similarly, through baptism into Christ's body these early Christians were secure, even if they faced death.

b) *1 Peter 4:6*. Here the apostle refers to believers who, though physically dead, were alive to God in glory, so that death had not deprived them of salvation. The gospel had been preached to them before their death, so that the judgment due to them as sinners was accomplished 'in the flesh', that is, while they were in the world.

Clearly, then, purgatory finds no support whatsoever in the Bible. To those who believe in Jesus Christ an abundant entrance is given, not into purgatory but into the everlasting kingdom of our Lord and Saviour Jesus Christ (2 Peter 1:11). Those, however, who die without Christ will be punished, says Paul, 'with everlasting destruction from the presence of the Lord' (2 Thess. 1:9). Hell, not purgatory, awaits unbelievers at death, immediately and eternally. A verse written by Rev. Griffith Jones, Llanddowror, and included as part of an appendix to his Catechism, is as relevant today as it was in the eighteenth century:

> *Think how death hastens, Judgment comes apace,*
> *And heaven or hell will shortly be thy place*
> *(For Purgatory's a mere dream, nor can*
> *The prayers of priests redeem a sinful man).*[6]

Second probation

Another theory gaining wide acceptance, especially among Jehovah's Witnesses, is that of a 'second probation'. Briefly, this sect teaches that in the 'resurrection of judgment' those people who wanted to do right, but previously lacked the knowledge of God's purposes, will be brought back to paradise – earth – where they will be instructed in the truth. If they obey then, according to The Watch Tower, they will inherit life. This is a more refined form of the 'sec-

---

6. *The Christian Faith, or The Apostles' Creed Scripturally Explained by Questions and Answers* (1762), p.73.

ond-chance' doctrine, and it illustrates how far these Bible students have themselves departed from the Bible. For example, the passage in question (John 5:28,29) assumes that the destinies of people are already decided. Further, in the light of passages like John 3:18-21, the division between believers and unbelievers cannot be altered after death; indeed, in this respect verse 18 is conclusive: 'He that believeth on him is not condemned; but he that believeth not is condemned already, because he hath not believed in the name of the only begotten son of God.'

Now that we have seen the meaning of the relevant biblical words, and considered, albeit briefly, certain objections and modifications to the orthodox doctrine of hell, we will turn to a consideration of what hell is like.

8
Hell
Its nature and duration

How does the New Testament describe hell? To answer this question we shall group together and expound some of the biblical descriptions of hell under two main headings: separation and punishment.

1. Separation

Paul's statement in 2 Thessalonians 1:9, that unbelievers 'shall be punished with everlasting destruction from the presence of the Lord, and from the glory of his power', underlines the fact that *separation* is an essential feature of hell. The verb 'punished' here means 'to pay a penalty', which is then specified as 'everlasting destruction'. Although this phrase is found nowhere else in the New Testament, it is a phrase which has been used to support the theory of annihilation. However, the Greek word *olethros* (translated 'destruction' in the Authorized Version) is qualified in an important way by the adjective *aiōnios* ('eternal'), which serves to stress the idea of duration rather than extinction. Furthermore, the phrase is immediately amplified in the following words, 'from the presence of the Lord, and from the glory of his power'. It is not extinction that is taught here, but rather a definite severance on the part of unbelievers from the presence and glory of Christ, which is the opposite of everlasting life. Originally the Greek word here translated 'power' was used to describe the authority and power exercised by magistrates (while its related adjective *ischuros* was used of an army or a fortress). Unbelievers, says the apostle Paul, will be separated from the splendour and glory of this power which belongs to Christ inherently, and which He uses especially on behalf of the elect to effect their salvation and glorification.

Our Lord also uses this principle of separation to describe the nature of hell. At the last day, for example, He will show great wrath towards the unbelieving despite their gifts and miraculous works, saying, 'I never knew you: depart from me, ye that work iniquity' (Matt. 7:23). 'They that would not *come to* Him to be saved', remarks Matthew Henry, 'must *depart from* Him to be damned. To *depart from* Christ is the very hell of hell; it is the foundation of all the misery of the damned, to be cut off from all hope of benefit from Christ and His mediation.'[1]

Later in Matthew's Gospel we find our Lord's words, 'Then shall he say also unto them on the left hand, Depart from me, ye cursed, into everlasting fire, prepared for the devil and his angels' (Matt. 25:41). Here separation is shown to be the exact opposite of inheriting 'the kingdom' (v.34) and 'eternal life' (v.46). To depart from Christ does not mean that in hell sinners are banished from the presence of God, for God is omnipresent; it does mean, however, that they are separated from the presence of His love. To be in the presence of God without a Saviour is to be in hell, for our God is a consuming fire (Heb. 12:29).

God's love and kindness towards mankind mean that unbelievers can live happy, meaningful lives here, being well-provided for by God in His providence. In expounding part of the section on Providence in the *Westminster Confession of Faith*, A. A. Hodge writes:

Thus also the providential government of God over mankind in general is subordinate as a means to an end to His gracious providence toward His Church,

---

1. *Matthew Henry's Commentary* (Marshall, Morgan & Scott, 1953), vol.5, p.97.

whereby He gathers it out of every people and nation, and makes all things work together for good to those who are called according to His purpose . . . The history of redemption through all its dispensations, Patriarchal, Abrahamic, Mosaic, and Christian, is the key to the philosophy of human history in general. The race is preserved, continents and islands are settled with inhabitants, nations are elevated to empire, philosophy and the practical arts, civilization and liberty are advanced, that the Church, the Lamb's bride, may be perfected in all her members and adorned for her Husband.[2]

Thus there is a special care that the Lord shows towards His believing people, and for this reason unbelievers benefit greatly from the presence of the church in the world. During World War II my father worked on the railway, and for part of the time he helped to move British and, later, American soldiers quite regularly. After being away from home for two or three days he would return with a bag full of 'goodies' that excited us as children; the chocolates, sweets, wrapped cream biscuits and chewing-gum were all displayed on the table for us to see and share. My father was not an American, nor was he a soldier, but he benefited greatly from the American presence in our country.

This is a picture of God's dealings with the world. Unbelievers are not part of the living church of Jesus Christ; yet they benefit greatly from God's love towards His church. Here in this world unbelievers can be happy and can find enjoyment and fulfilment in God-given relationships and responsibilties; but in hell unbelievers will be deprived of all these expressions of divine love and kindness. Hell, therefore, is separation from the love and favour of God, so that the ungodly in hell will be exposed to His wrath without any mercy at all.

2. A.A. Hodge, *The Confession of Faith* (Banner of Truth, 1958), p.101.

2. Punishment

The New Testament also emphasizes the fact that sinners are *punished* in hell by God.

In Matthew 25:46 the Lord Jesus describes the fate of the ungodly as that of 'everlasting punishment'. The significance of the adjective *aiōnios* will be considered later, but I want at this point to indicate the significance of the Greek word *kolasis*, translated 'punishment'. The Watch Tower translates the word as 'cutting-off', adapting it rather conveniently to support their doctrine of annihilation; but this translation is wrong. Similarly some evangelicals have insisted that the word means death and annihilation, not punishment; such a death, they argue, is eternal only in its effect.

The word is used in its verbal form in Acts 4:21, where we are told that the Sanhedrin tried in vain to obtain evidence on which they could lawfully *punish* (*not* annihilate) Peter and John. It is also used in 2 Peter 2:9, with reference to the unjust being reserved *in punishment* until the final judgment. In this latter reference it is important to note that the verb is in the present tense and the passive voice, giving the sense 'are being punished'. It means that the ungodly are being punished both in the world and in hell, but after the final judgment they will receive the full measure of their punishment. Again, the word occurs in 1 John 4:18, where we read that 'fear has to do with punishment' (NIV).

'Punishment', then, and not 'cutting-off', must be regarded as the correct translation of the word *kolasis* in Matthew 25:46, and it is this concept of punishment that is used by the Lord Jesus and by the apostle Peter to describe the nature and purpose of hell's sufferings.

Today the idea of punishment is frowned upon. Capital punishment has been abolished and prison sentences are regarded as reformatory and educative rather than punitive. Mr James Jardine, chairman of the Police Federation, speaking a few years ago to police officers in Matlock Bath, Derbyshire, said: 'Long ago people in power stopped talking about the punishment of crime and began to talk of treatment, as if every young thug was sick and in need of a prescription from the chemist. Discipline has disappeared in our schools and the concept of parental responsibility went out with the Ark.'[3] Within education corporal punishment has been withdrawn, and parents are discouraged by psychiatrists and sociologists from punishing their children. Religious education specialists tell us we should withhold biblical material, whether stories or teaching, if it includes suggestions of violence or death – and this in spite of the fact that children are extremely knowledgeable about cowboys, TV 'thrillers', football hooliganism, IRA atrocities and, more recently, the street violence in several British cities! Some children also see their mothers and other relatives beaten regularly in their homes by cruel and often drunken men.

How do we communicate the truth of eternal punishment in this contemporary situation? Where do we begin? We must begin with God and His Word, for punishment is an integral part of God's justice. His rectorial justice has instituted a moral government in the world, and God decrees that this should be exercised, through parents, magistrates, governments and kings, etc. But there is another aspect to His justice, namely, His distributive justice, in which He executes His law and distributes rewards and punishments to both humans and angels. In His wrath He inflicts penalties justly on sinners, through parents, civil authorities, and even by means of the actual consequences of our own sins, as well as through various material and physical judgments. Hell, however, is the climax of this distributive or retributive justice. Rather than being offensive and an unnecessary addendum to life, it is

3. *The Daily Telegraph*, 14 July 1981, p.2.

the continuation of a principle God already upholds within the world, and without which social life would deteriorate into anarchy.

What constitutes the punishment of hell?

Our Lord tells us that the soul and, eventually, the body are involved in punishment; consider, for example, Matthew 10:28 and Mark 9:43-45. Writing early in eighteenth-century Wales, the Rev. Jenkin Jones remarked that hell's punishment will be terrible not only 'because of the loss the sinner will suffer in the body and soul there, but also the loss he will suffer in *every* part of *both* body and soul. Not only will the unbeliever be in hell, but hell will be in him too'[4] – in his conscience, in his body and in his soul.

Conscience will inflict its own punishment on sinners in hell. John Flavel writes:

> Conscience, which should have been the sinner's curb on earth, becomes the whip that must lash his soul in hell . . . That which was the seat and centre of all guilt, now becomes the seat and the centre of all torments . . . should the Lord let a sinner's conscience fly upon him with rage . . . it would put him into a hell upon earth . . . But he keeps a hand of restraint upon them . . . But no sooner is the Christless soul turned out of the body . . . but the conscience is roused and put into a rage never to be appeased any more.[5]

The reference in Mark 9:44 to 'their worm dieth not' is regarded as a reference to a condemning conscience which persists throughout eternity.

Punishment in hell is also described as 'everlasting fire' (Matt. 18:8), 'the fire' that 'is not quenched' (Mark 9:46), 'flaming fire' (2 Thess. 1:8), 'eternal fire' (Jude 7). We are told that 'the smoke of their torment ascendeth up for ever

---

4. Thomas Vincent, *Christ's Certain and Sudden Appearance to Judgment* (1667) – quoted from the Welsh translation by Jenkin Jones, *Dydd y Farn Fawr* (1727), p.161.
5. *The Works of John Flavel* (Banner of Truth, 1968), vol.3, p.137.

and ever' (Rev. 14:11; 19:3). Dives was also 'in torments' and 'in this flame' (Luke 16:23,24), while the devil, the beast and the prophet 'shall be tormented day and night for ever and ever' (Rev. 20:10). Thomas Boston describes these torments as being universal (that is, every part of the person is affected), manifold, uninterrupted, unpitied and eternal.[6] In addition to pangs of conscience, references like Matthew 8:12 and 13:50, Mark 9:43-48, Luke 16:23-28, Revelation 14:10 and 21:8 underline other subjective punishments, such as anguish, despair, weeping and gnashing of teeth, which will constitute an essential part of hell's punishment after death for unbelievers.

Hell-fire

How literal is the fire of hell? John Owen, the Puritan divine, was clear as to his interpretation of it: 'By "hell-fire" we understand nothing but the "wrath of God" for sin; into whose hands it is a fearful thing to fall, our God being a consuming fire.'[7] Jonathan Edwards also stresses that the all-important feature of heaven and hell is God Himself. God makes hell and He is hell: 'God will be the hell of one and the heaven of the other . . . 'Tis the infinite almighty God that shall become the fire of the furnace'[8] and, figuratively speaking, the wrath of God is a consuming fire. When pressed to answer whether hell-fire is literal or figurative, he replies that the symbol is 'very probably literal',[9] for verses like Matthew 10:28, he suggests, require it. Berkhof lacks Edwards's assurance and says we cannot be sure, but 'there will be some positive punishment corresponding to our bodies'.[10] For Herman Hoeksema terms like

6. Thomas Boston, *Human Nature in its Fourfold State* (Banner of Truth, 1964), pp.487-91.
7. *The Works of John Owen* (Banner of Truth, 1966), vol.12, p.147.
8. Gerstner, *Jonathan Edwards on Heaven and Hell* , pp.57,53.
9. ibid., p.55.
10. L. Berkhof, *Systematic Theology*, p.736.

'fire' and 'worm' indicate 'an existence in unspeakable suffering of both body and soul'.[11]

It is worth noting the caution and emphasis of men like Owen and Edwards, namely, that God Himself is a consuming fire to the ungodly. This God-centred approach needs to be stressed in our preaching of hell. In his commentary on 2 Thessalonians, Hendriksen issues what is a much needed warning. With reference to the phrase 'in flaming fire' (2 Thess. 1:7) he says:

> To speak about a 'mere' symbol in such connections is never right. The reality which answers to the symbol is always far more terrible (or far more glorious) than the symbol itself. Human language is stretched almost to its breaking-point in order to convey the terrible character of the coming of the Lord in relation to the wicked.[12]

That this 'everlasting fire' involves considerable suffering is emphasized in the New Testament; for instance, in Revelation 20:10 we read that Satan will be 'tormented day and night for ever and ever'! Both in the realm of the body and the soul unbelievers will suffer the fire of God's wrath without being themselves consumed, just as in a very different situation the three Hebrews in Babylon stood inside the burning furnace without being burnt in any way (Dan. 3).

Our Lord also teaches that there will be *degrees of punishment* in hell. In Matthew 10:14, for example, referring to the custom amongst the Jews of removing the dust from their clothes and sandals after travelling through a pagan area, the Lord warns that even a Jewish city or house can be unclean if it refuses to welcome the gospel. When people refuse to hear the gospel, He tells the disciples, they too must indicate that such people are pagans by turning

---

11. Herman Hoeksema, *Reformed Dogmatics* (Grand Rapids: Reformed Free Publishing Association, 1973), pp.866-7.
12. William Hendriksen, *1 & 2 Thessalonians* (Banner of Truth, 1972), pp.159-60.

from them and shaking the dust from off their feet (cf. Acts 13:50,51). Those who spurn the gospel are here warned that they will be punished more severely in the final judgment than the notoriously wicked cities of Sodom and Gomorrah.

This point is reiterated in Matthew 11:22-24 with reference to the unbelief of the people living in Capernaum. Despite our Lord's great Galilean ministry, involving a lengthy period of residence and ministry there and including numerous miracles, the inhabitants had not repented. These mighty works performed by Christ amongst them should have caused them to repent, and so the Lord warns them:

> And thou, Capernaum, which art exalted into heaven, shall be brought down to hell: for if the mighty works which have been done in thee, had been done in Sodom, it would have remained until this day. But I say unto you, That it shall be more tolerable for the land of Sodom in the day of judgment, than for thee.

This truth He explains in greater detail in Luke 12:47, 48: 'For unto whomsoever much is given, of him shall be much required . . .' Here we can underline the following principles. First of all, ignorance, though it is inexcusable and punishable in the most dreadful manner, will nevertheless be punished less severely in hell. This is an important principle, for it is suggested by some believers, and stated officially by Jehovah's Witnesses, that sinners are unworthy of punishment until they hear and reject the Word. If this were true, it would be a powerful reason for disengaging the church from its task of world mission. But this cannot possibly be the case; it is clear from the Scriptures that all men are already condemned in Adam and will be judged and punished righteously by the Lord.

Secondly, increased knowledge implies increased responsibility: the greater the light, the greater will be the liability and punishment. In his comments on Matthew 25:46 Bishop Ryle asks:

> Who shall describe the misery of eternal punishment? It is something utterly indescribable and inconceivable. The eternal pain of the body; the eternal sting of an accusing conscience; the eternal society of none but the wicked, the devil and his angels; the eternal remembrance of opportunities neglected and Christ despised; the eternal prospect of a weary, hopeless future – all this is misery indeed . . . And yet this picture is nothing compared to the reality.[13]

Eternal

Let us now consider the *eternity* of hell's punishment, doing so against the background of the contemporary controversy.

Aiōnios

First of all, we need to consider the meaning and significance of the Greek word *aiōnios* in the phrase 'everlasting punishment' (Matt. 25:46). This word and its cognates are used 71 times in the New Testament. While it sometimes denotes an 'age' or an indefinite period of time, it is used in the majority of cases in the New Testament in the sense of 'everlasting'. For example, both in Romans 16:26 and in 1 Timothy 1:17 the word expresses the eternity of God; in Hebrews 9:14 it describes the eternal Spirit, and in Revelation 1:18 the endless reign of Christ. On 51 occasions the word is used to describe the unending bliss of the redeemed in heaven. The fact that this same word is used twice in Matthew 25:46, both to describe the duration of 'everlasting life' and to describe the duration of hell, means that one cannot escape the conclusion that when descriptive of hell it has the sense of 'everlasting'.

13. J.C. Ryle, *Expository Thoughts on the Gospels: Matthew* (James Clarke, 1954), pp.344-5.

Augustine has a helpful statement on this discussion of the meaning of *aiōnios:*

> What a thing it is, to account eternal punishment to be a fire of long duration, and eternal life to be without end, since Christ comprised both in that very same place, in one and the same sentence, saying, 'These shall go away into everlasting punishment: but the righteous into life eternal'! If both are eternal, either both must be understood to be lasting with an end, or both perpetual without an end. For like is related to like; on the one side, eternal punishment, on the other, eternal life. But to say in one and the same sentence, life eternal shall be without end, punishment eternal shall have an end, were too absurd: whence, since the eternal life of the saints shall be without end, punishment eternal, too, shall doubtless have no end to those whose it shall be.[14]

Writing much later than Augustine, the Rev. E.H. Pusey, Professor of Hebrew at Oxford, expressed his exasperation in 1880 with the way people were playing fast and loose with the inspired words of Scripture: 'They who deny that any of the words used of future punishment in Holy Scripture express eternity, would do well to consider, whether there is any way, in which Almighty God *could* have expressed it, which they would have accepted, as meaning it!'[15]

The conclusion, however, that *aiōnios* means 'everlasting' in relation to hell, is questioned by the advocates of conditional immortality, who argue that eternal punishment is eternal in its effects but not in its suffering. On this interpretation conditionalists deny the immortality of the soul and affirm the annihilation of the unbelieving at death.

Jehovah's Witnesses go further than Seventh Day Adventists, by denying that there is any evidence in the

14. Augustine, *De Civitate Dei*, xxi. 23.
15. E.H. Pusey, *What is of Faith as to Eternal Punishment?* (James Parker, 1880), p.44.

Bible for life or consciousness or activity after death, apart from the 144,000 who are now in heaven. But this position can be easily refuted by Old Testament references: for example, Psalms 16:8-11; 17:15; 49:15; 73:24-26; Isaiah 14:9-17; 25:8, and Ezekiel 32:21. The command against consulting evil spirits is also a strong argument for immortality and, of course, numerous New Testament references are a distinct embarrassment to the Watch Tower Society: for example, Matthew 17:3; Luke 12:4,5; Philippians 1:21-23; 2 Corinthians 5:1,6,8; and 1 Thessalonians 5:10.

The Bible consistently speaks of suffering and loss rather than annihilation after death for unbelievers. Furthermore, the fact that there are degrees of punishment in hell is incompatible with annihilation. Coupled with the force and use of the adjective *aiōnios* and the fact that the character of sinners in hell does not change, thereby incurring God's wrath eternally, we must conclude that annihilation has no biblical warrant whatsoever.

Bishop Ryle's summary of the biblical position deserves to be mentioned here:

> The misery of the lost, and the blessedness of the saved, are both alike for ever: let no man deceive us on this point. It is clearly revealed in Scripture: the eternity of God, and heaven, and hell, all stand on the same foundation. As surely as God is eternal, so surely is heaven an endless day without night, and hell an endless night without day.[16]

The concept of eternity as being timeless is difficult for humans, and for this and other reasons we can agree with Jonathan Edwards's statement that we have no positive idea of hell's eternity. He says, 'It is that duration that has no end', and then, after listing several negative and positive qualities of hell, he repeats, 'eternal means there will be no end'.[17] Again, in struggling to explain the eternity

---

16. Ryle, *Expository Thoughts: Matthew*, p.344.
17. Gerstner, *Jonathan Edwards on Heaven and Hell*, p.73.

of hell, Edwards adds that 'all arithmetic here fails, no rules of multiplication can reach the amount, for there is no end'.[18]

Thomas Boston was naturally compelled to use the time-category to describe the eternity of the unbeliever's misery in hell. He makes two brief statements concerning it: first of all, it has a beginning; secondly, it will never have an end. 'Wherefore eternity, which is before us,' writes Boston, 'is a duration that has a beginning but no end.' He then qualifies that statement: 'It is a beginning without a middle, a beginning without an end . . . There is no end of it: while God is, it shall be.'[19]

The position of John Stott quoted earlier, however, is an unsound one at this point. While we acknowledge the difficulty of describing eternity, as did Jonathan Edwards, we are not warranted to introduce the possibility of eventual hope or annihilation for unbelievers after death. For this possibility there is no biblical basis whatsoever.

The eternity of hell's sufferings should make us the more zealous and eager to tell people of the only One who is able to rescue them. Do we shrink from declaring these solemn truths? Does the thought of hell displease us? Remember that God will be glorified even through the eternal sufferings of unbelievers in hell. His injured majesty will be vindicated. In his famous sermon on 'Sinners in the Hands of an angry God' Jonathan Edwards says, 'God hath had it on His heart to show to angels and men, both how excellent His love is, and also how terrible His wrath is.'[20] What is supreme in the purpose of God in the election and reprobation of men is His own glory, and hell also will glorify the justice, power and wrath of God throughout eternity. In the meantime it is our responsibility to pray and work for the salvation of sinners before such awful punishment overtakes them.

18. *The Works of Jonathan Edwards*, vol.2, p.883.
19. Boston, *Human Nature in its Fourfold State*, p.495.
20. *The Works of Jonathan Edwards*, vol.2, p.10.

9
Is the Soul Immortal?

Does the Bible teach that the soul is immortal? Increasingly throughout the century a negative answer has been given to the question. Over fifty years ago, Archbishop William Temple wrote that, according to the New Testament,

> God alone is immortal and that he offers immortality to men not universally but conditionally.

Norman Snaith, the former Methodist scholar, declared in 1954:

> I find nowhere in the Bible any doctrine of the necessary . . . immortality of the soul in the sense that there is a part of every man which can never die . . . Sin will at the last be destroyed, and with it all that cling to it.

The New Testament scholar, Oscar Cullman, wrote in 1958:

> For the first Christians the soul is not intrinsically immortal, but rather became so only through the resurrection of Jesus and through faith in him . . .

In a radio address on Immortality from Baronmunster in 1958, Karl Barth insisted that

> Immortality cannot be the acquisition of man [of any man] except as a new and unmerited gift, a free gift from him who alone possesses it, who alone by nature is immortal.

A year later, J. Stafford Wright said,

> There is no text in Scripture which indicates that God cannot annihilate the human personality.

In the *New Bible Commentary Revised* (IVP), Robin E. Nixon wrote on Matthew 10:28,

The soul in biblical thought is not immortal, except when new life is conferred upon it through Christ (1 Tim. 6:16; 2 Tim. 1:10). Hell is therefore the place of its destruction, as Gehenna, the Valley of Hinnon, was of the rubbish of Jerusalem.[1]

Professor Alan Richardson in his *Theological Word Book of the Bible* expressed his view more fiercely: 'The illusion of natural or inherent immortality is the serpent's lie.'

Five of the seven quotations above are from liberal scholars, so their theological presuppositions and conclusions are suspect. On the other hand, Nixon and Wright were Anglican evangelicals. This is interesting for it was amongst Anglican evangelicals in particular that the theory of conditional immortality has been most popular during the twentieth century in Britain. More recently, other evangelicals in the Anglican church have openly questioned or denied the immortality of the soul; these include John Wenham and John Stott. The latter writes: '. . . the immortality – and therefore indestructibility – of the soul is a Greek not a biblical concept. According to Scripture only God possesses immortality in himself (1 Tim. 1:17; 6:16); he reveals and gives it to us through the gospel (2 Tim. 1:10).'[2] But support for conditional immortality has broadened recently to include representatives of other denominations. Arthur Custance, for example, wrote in 1979:

> The soul is only contingently immortal, as sustained by God . . . Immortality of the soul is a Greek invention, not biblical revelation. Luther considered the doctrine of the immortality of the soul as the last of the five cardinal errors of the papal church.[3]

1. All the foregoing quotations are used in the editorial of *Resurrection*, Jan.-March 1987, p.2. The books quoted are Temple's *Nature, Man and God*; Snaith's *I Believe In . . .* and Cullman's *Immortality of the Soul or Resurrection of the Dead*, and then Stafford Wright's *What is Man?*
2. Edwards and Stott, *Essentials*, p.316.
3. Custance, *The Sovereignty of Grace*, p.354

The challenge of these various quotations will now be faced in the rest of the chapter.

Briefly, the conclusions of conditionalists are wrong. However, the advocates of the soul's immortality or continuity after physical death have not been sufficiently biblical in the way they describe, and marshal the evidence in support of, this doctrine. This weakness has in turn served to increase the plausibility of the conditionalist position.

Definitions

The word 'immortality' occurs only five times in the Authorized Version of the Bible where it translates two different Greek words, namely, *athanasia* and *aphtharsia.*

Athanasia literally means 'no death', immunity from death; it is a never-ending existence or a state of being incapable of death. The word is used in a redemptive, resurrection context in 1 Corinthians 15 verses 53 and 54. These verses tell us that when the bodies of unbelievers will be raised and changed, they will thus be immune from death for ever. The same word is also used in relation to God in 1 Timothy 6:16: 'who alone hath immortality'. In addition to endless existence, 'the concept *immortality . . .* means that God is life's never-failing Fountain'.[4] In this double sense, only God has immortality in and of Himself. We can add another point here. All men have been created in the image of God and are thereby capable of unending existence even in hell; it is believers, however, who exclusively enjoy eternal life in the sense of the duration, fulness and blessedness of life which has been brought to light through the gospel (2 Tim. 1:16). 'For the believer', concludes Hendriksen, 'immortality is therefore a redemptive concept. It is *everlasting salvation.* For God it is *eternal blessedness.* But while the believer *has received* immortality, as one receives a drink of water from a fountain, God

---

4. William Hendriksen, *1 & 2 Timothy and Titus* (Banner of Truth, 1959), pp.207-8.

has it. It belongs to his very being. He *is* himself the Fountain.'[5]

The second Greek word translated as immortality is *aphtharsia*; this word is used in Romans 2:7, 1 Corinthians 15:42,50,52,53-54 and 2 Timothy 1:10. Literally, it means 'no corruption' and immunity from decay. In the first reference, immortality has a future reference and is associated with 'glory and honour and . . . eternal life'. The picture of sowing and reaping is used in 1 Corinthians 15:42. The bodies of believers are corruptible and subject to decay in this life. Although their bodies die and disintegrate yet at the resurrection the bodies of Christians will be 'raised in incorruption' and will never decay again. Verses 50,52,53-54 express the necessity and certainty of the bodies of believers being raised immortal and imperishable. Here, in 2 Timothy 1:10, writes Donald Guthrie,

> The whole range of Christ's work is envisaged as an accomplished fact . . . By linking immortality (aphtharsia) with LIFE, the apostle defines more closely the quality of life. Because Christians possess a life which cannot decay, anticipation of the accident of physical death can do nothing to destroy their confidence.[6]

Hendriksen adds: 'This is the immortality (cf. 1 Tim. 1:17) which in the gospel is promised to believers. It transcends by far mere endless existence or even endless conscious existence. The gospel of our Saviour Christ Jesus is far better than anything Plato ever excogitated!'[7]

We now need to mention some implications of the New Testament use of the words *athanasia* and *aphtharsia*. First, immortality means much more than the continuity and survival of the soul at death; it emphasizes, in particular, full participation in eternal life. Secondly, 1 Corinthians 15:52-54 indicates that immortality is given to believers when the Lord raises their bodies from the graves

5. ibid., p.208.
6. Donald Guthrie, *The Pastoral Epistles* (Tyndale, 1957), p.130.
7. Hendriksen, *1 & 2 Timothy and Titus*, p.234.

at His parousia. Immortality and resurrection are inseparably related for *anathasia* and *aphtharsia* are used in a
physical but redemptive and future context. Thirdly, the
gift of immortality depends on an individual's relationship
to Christ, not to Adam; it arises from our union with
Christ, not merely from our creation by God.

The advocates of the theory of conditional immortality
are right in drawing attention to the redemptive and resurrection context of immortality. They are wrong, however, in
concluding that unbelievers do not have a soul which sur-
vives death. The orthodox doctrine of the soul's immortality is biblical but we have not always described and
expressed it with sufficient distinctness or scriptural preci-
sion. For example, rather than using the term immortality
it is more precise to refer to the soul's continuity and survival after death. Unwittingly, we may have helped to make
the conditionalist argument more plausible by our loose
and wrong usage of the term 'immortality' with regard to
the soul. Before marshaling the biblical evidence for the
survival of the souls of unbelievers after death, we must
refer to the charge made by conditionalists that the conti-
nuity/survival of the soul is a Greek not a biblical concept.

The fact that some Christians in the past formulated
the doctrine of the soul under the dominant influence of
Greek philosophy rather than clear biblical teaching is
acknowledged. In varying degrees, consciously or uncon-
sciously, we are all influenced by the secular religious
thinking of the age in which we live and proponents of the
soul's immortality are no exception. But neither are conditionalists exempt from strong secular influences predis-
posing them to accept, and argue in support of, their
theory. While conditionalists frequently charge orthodox
defenders of the soul's continuity of being duped by Greek
philosophy, they forget that they themselves were powerfully influenced in the nineteenth century by secular theories of punishment and more liberal approaches to the

Bible. A ferment occured within Christendom in the middle of the last century involving a liberalizing of biblical doctrines such as the Atonement, Scripture, eternal punishment and the soul's immortality. Some evangelicals joined forces with liberals in this secularizing process; at the same time, most of the more established cults which teach annihilation emerged during this period. The seed-bed, therefore, of the contemporary theories of annihilation and conditional immortality is a dubious one indeed.

The usual objection made by conditionalists is that Christianity derived its doctrine of resurrection from the Old Testament Scriptures and inter-testamental writings but borrowed the concept of immortality from extra-biblical sources, especially Greek philosophers like Plato. Murray J. Harris declares that this claim by conditionalists is 'indefensible' and that the 'Judaism of the apostolic era knew both conceptions'.[8] Recent research by H.C.C. Cavallin in this respect is conclusive. After a detailed and extensive study of Jewish literature between 200 BC and AD 100, he concludes:

> statements on an immortality of the soul which excludes the resurrection of the body are almost as common as those which explicitly state the resurrection of the body, and the same proportions can be asserted for statements on the soul's life after death with exclusion of the body and texts which state the resurrection without explicit reference to the body.[9]

What this research establishes is that the doctrine of the immortality, or rather the continuity, of the soul was articulated and taught in inter-testamental Jewish writings and long before the New Testament was written. This doctrine, therefore, was not originally derived from Greek philosophy

8. *Themelios*, vol. 1: 2, Spring 1976, pp.52-3.
9. H.C.C. Cavallin, *Life After Death. Paul's Argument for the Resurrection of the Dead in 1 Corinthians 15. Part I: An enquiry into the Jewish Background* (Lund, 1974), p.200.

by the early Apologists and Church Fathers in the post-apostolic period. Furthermore, a strong case can be established that in the period 200 B C –A D 100 the Jewish belief in the soul's survival was grounded more in Hebrew thought than in the early influences of Greek philosophy. 'No longer', affirms Murray Harris, 'can anyone maintain that "resurrection" is Hebraic and "immortality" Greek.' [10]

Quite frequently we are told that the Bible 'assumes' the doctrine of the continuing and endless conscious existence of the soul after death. Louis Berkhof, for example, says that the Bible assumes this doctrine 'very much as it does that of the existence of God, that is, it assumes this as an undisputed postulate'.[11] The Bible, therefore, does not set out to 'prove' the doctrine in any formal way. Confirming this point, Donald MacDonald writes:

> . . . if not directly taught in the Old Testament, [the doctrine] was assumed as self-evident truth, immanent in the consciousness of the people . . . Though the passages which clearly articulate the doctrine are comparatively few, they are not exceptional or alien to the general climate of truth taught. On the contrary, so obviously are they of a piece with the whole body of Old Testament teaching that we can assert that the fact of immortality is assumed, and only on the basis of this assumption can we appreciate the self-consistency and unitary nature of the truth taught. Accept this assumption which . . . becomes specific in certain passages and you can make sense of the whole . . . [12]

While both Berkhof and MacDonald are right, at the same time we understand the frustration of conditionalists who demand clearer and convincing biblical support for this doctrine. However, before turning to this clearer evidence, two further points need to be stressed.

First of all, the focus of the Bible is not so much on the

10. *Themelios*, vol. 1:2, Spring 1976, p.53.
11. L. Berkhof, *Systematic Theology*, p.674.
12. *The Banner of Truth*, April 1987, pp.17-18.

'soul' but on the human person. In the words of Paul Helm, the Bible 'does not teach that at death a person permanently loses his body as a butterfly permanently loses its chrysalis, but that the redeemed will receive a "spiritual body"'[13] Again, nowhere does the Bible suggest that the soul is independent of God's sustaining activity. The soul cannot exist either in heaven or hell apart from God's energizing support.

Secondly, the Bible *implies* as well as assumes the fact of the soul's conscious, unending continuity in the afterlife. For example, God's future judgment of sinners, the consequent reward or punishment of people, and the command against consulting evil spirits and the dead all imply the continuity of the soul consciously and permanently beyond death.

Bearing in mind the progressive nature of biblical revelation, we can now consider further evidence for the continuous, conscious existence of the soul beyond death.

Image of God

Man is a unique creation for he has been made in the image of God (Gen. 1:27; 5:1; cf. v. 2-3, 9:6). The likeness, therefore, is not between humans and animals as evolutionists insist but rather between humans and God Himself. Our likeness to God can be described in several ways. Like God, for example, humans are rational, thinking beings with a personality and consciousness. In addition, God, who is Himself a moral and holy Being, also created humans with a moral nature capable of discerning between right and wrong. Man's likeness to God extends even further. As God is spirit (John 4:24), to be created in His image means that all humans are created with a spiritual dimension and capacity which continues beyond physical death. Berkhof is justified in underlining the significance of this truth:

13. Helm, *The Last Things*, p.118.

. . . the Old Testament represents man as created in the image of God, created for life and not for mortality. In distinction from the brute, he possesses a life that transcends time and already contains within itself a pledge of immortality. He is made for communion with God . . . and God has set eternity in his heart . . . [14]

We can now turn to other scriptural references relevant to the doctrine of the soul's survival beyond the grave.

Ecclesiastes 3:11, although not conclusive, is an interesting statement, particularly the words, 'also he hath set the world in their heart. . .' Verses 1-15 in the chapter illustrate the sovereign rule of God over people. Verse 11 records that God 'hath made every thing beautiful in his time' and it is a reference to the divine purpose and harmony which cover all areas of life. People are able to appreciate this providence only because God 'set the world in their heart . . .' But the word 'world' is a poor translation as the Hebrew *olãm* is best rendered as 'eternity'. Is the statement confined to a 'faculty of appreciating the lasting import of things'[15] or does it include a desire for eternal things which in turn implies a spiritual dimension and nature in men?

Verse 21 must be considered briefly before leaving the chapter. From verses 16-22 we are informed that even man's wickedness is overruled in the Lord's sovereign purpose. Verse 19 teaches that there are similarities between men and beasts but nowhere is this seen more clearly than in their death (v.20). However, verse 21 draws attention to an important dissimilarity between humans and animals, namely, the fact that 'the spirit of man . . . goeth upward and the spirit of the beast . . . goeth downward to the earth'. We will not press the statement too far except to note man's spirit, unlike that of the animal, is directed beyond the grave with the strong implication of continuity and life.

14. L. Berkhof, *Systematic Theology*, p.675.
15. H. C. Leupold, *Exposition of Ecclesiastes* (Baker, 1952), p.90.

Ecclesiastes 12:7 is another statement which merits attention. Several pictures are used in the earlier verses to describe the frailty and ageing process of humans but the climax is reached in verse 7 with the terse reminder that man's body returns to the earth. Notice the distinction and contrast here between man's body and spirit; the latter will 'return unto God, who gave it'. It is not reabsorption into God which is taught here but 'a coming into judgment'[16] which denotes personal survival as well as accountability. A similar statement that there is 'a spirit in man' occurs in Job 32:8.

Various Hebrew and Greek words are used in the Bible to refer to man's 'soul' or 'spirit'. The Hebrew *nephesh* occurs 754 times in the Hebrew Bible and is translated in thirty different ways in the Authorized Version. While it has a figurative usage in places, *nephesh* refers more often either to the principle of life or to man's soul. Another word is *ruach* which is found 361 times in the Hebrew and Aramaic forms in the Hebrew Bible and translated in twelve different ways in the Authorized Version but with a range of meanings. It is *ruach* which is used in Ecclesiastes 12:7 and Job 32:8. The Greek *psuchē* is found over a hundred times in the New Testament and translated in the Authorized Version as soul, life, mind, heart, etc. Arndt and Gingrich define it as (a) the life principle in man and animals, (b) earthly life itself and (c) the soul or inner self which transcends physical life.[17] In addition to *psuche, pneuma* is used in the New Testament just over 400 times and Arndt and Gingrich define it in six related ways ranging from wind to the human self and disincarnate souls.[18]

The Old Testament usage of *she'ol* and its implications both for the soul and the doctrine of eternal punishment will be referred to in the next chapter, but one final

16. ibid., p.287.
17. ibid., pp.901-2.
18. ibid., pp.680-5.

reference needs to be noted in conclusion, namely, Luke 16:19-31. Like s*he'ol*, this passage will be considered in more detail shortly but Murray J. Harris is correct in affirming that it is 'legitimate to deduce from the setting of this story the basic characteristics of the post mortem state of Christians and non-Christians'.[19] J. Paterson Smyth confirms the point: 'This is a direct statement about the invisible things themselves. Jesus is telling what happens after death.'[20] Here, a continuing conscious life after physical death is depicted for both believers and unbelievers in which they are represented as having memory, feelings and the capacity to think as well as speak. The whole passage, particularly verse 23, would be meaningless unless unbelievers have a soul which continues in hell after this life. However, it is more accurate to describe this teaching as the continuity, rather than the immortality, of the soul especially when unbelievers are in view.

19. *Themelios*, vol. 2:2, Jan. 1986, p.48.
20. J. Paterson Smyth, *The Gospel of the Hereafter* (Hodder & Stoughton), p.61.

10
Hell
More Objections Considered

We come now to consider in more detail the main arguments used recently by evangelicals in support of conditional immortality and annihilation. These arguments can be classified in three ways, namely, observational, exegetical and theological; the latter two arguments are more important and need to be examined in depth after we have briefly noted the observational argument.

1. Observational argument

Arthur Custance is one of several contemporary conditionalists who use this argument in order to question the doctrine of everlasting punishment:

> All too many of us who know the Lord are comparatively unmoved by any conscious awareness of the fate of the unsaved. We are not sufficiently concerned to seek to pluck out of the fire even though we pay lip service to a belief in everlasting punishment.[1]

Sadly, Custance is right. We assent to the doctrine of everlasting punishment but we are not gripped by its reality and awfulness. Instead of compassion, indifference characterizes our attitude towards the lost and we lack the sense of urgency which will constrain us to pray for, and witness to, unbelievers before they die and go to hell. We ought to repent of our sin in this matter and pray to the Lord for a heaven-given compassion and zeal for men and women. Nevertheless, the indifference of Christians to the destiny of unbelievers does not falsify the truth of the

1. Custance, *The Sovereignty of Grace*, p.315.

doctrine of everlasting punishment. This doctrine remains true whether or not Christians are zealous in warning the lost. On the other hand, John Wenham offers a helpful warning at this point to those who abandon the orthodox doctrine of hell:

> Beware of weakening zeal for the gospel. The gospel should be preached with passionate urgency. One who has believed that the alternative to faith in Christ is unending misery in hell may well find that the sudden loss of confidence in this doctrine will leave him deflated, with the edge of his evangelistic zeal impaired.[2]

2. Exegetical arguments

Writing recently in *Essentials*,[3] John Stott touches in detail on this exegetical argument by referring both to the language and also the imagery used in Scripture to characterize hell, especially that of fire.[4] The issue is stated clearly by Stott: 'will the final destiny of the impenitent be eternal conscious torment . . . or will it be a total annihilation of their being?'[5] Is everlasting punishment only 'a tradition which has to yield to the supreme authority of Scripture?'[6] We begin, therefore, by considering Stott's argument concerning the language of Scripture.

Language

His argument concerning language involves the claim that the vocabulary of 'destruction' often used to describe hell should be understood literally in the sense of 'extinction of being' rather than everlasting punishment.

a) *apollumi*

Stott rightly says that the commonest Greek word used in this context is the verb *apollumi* (destroy) and its cognate

2. J.W. Wenham, *The Enigma of Evil* (IVP, 1985), p.39.
3. Edwards and Stott, *Essentials*, pp.315-18.
4. ibid., pp.316-18.
5. ibid., p.314.
6. ibid., p.315.

noun meaning destruction. This Greek verb occurs 85 times in the New Testament and is translated variously as 'lose', 'perish' or 'destroy' in the Authorized Version.

Clearly, the word is used in the context of ordinary physical death as in Matthew 2:13; 12:14 and 27:4. This use of the word is not in dispute. But does this literal use of *apollumi* prove annihilation? Stott thinks it does and uses some smaller arguments in order to question the traditional doctrine. He uses, first, Matthew 10:28 and concludes: 'If to kill is to deprive the body of life, hell would seem to be the deprivation of both physical and spiritual life, that is, an extinction of being.'[7] The language is tentative but Stott rationalizes when he concludes that the literal meaning of the word demands extinction. Two points need to be made here. It is usual for some Hebrew/Greek words in Scripture to be used in different senses, therefore, one must be wary of imposing a fixed, literal interpretation upon the word 'destroy'. Another point is that in some contexts, Stott's use of this verb as meaning extinction would be absurd. In 2 Peter 3:6, for example, Peter says that 'the world . . . being overflowed with water, *perished* (*apōleto*). Rather than being made extinct, the world was in fact preserved and renewed by God (cf. Heb. 1:11-12). Again this same word, *apollumi* and its participles, is used several times in Luke 15 to describe the lost coin, the lost sheep and the prodigal son. Neither the coin nor the sheep nor the son was extinct or annihilated; rather, they were all lost.

Stott's next argument in support of a literal interpretation of 'destroy' is also questionable: 'It would seem strange', he writes, 'if people who are said to suffer destruction are in fact not destroyed.'[8] But is it so strange? Exodus 3:3 tells us of a burning bush which was not destroyed while Daniel 3 tells us of three godly young men

7. ibid., p.315.
8. ibid., p.316.

who were thrown into 'the burning fiery furnace' yet were not burnt or destroyed by the fire. Why cannot this, in principle, be true of eternal destruction and the awful spiritual fire of God's wrath?

Although not mentioned by Stott, there are other words used in the exegetical argument to support annihilation. We refer to them briefly.

b) *kolasis*

We have looked at this word already. It only needs to be added that the related Greek verk *koladzō* is frequently used by Xenophon and other classical Greek writers for 'punish' or 'chastise'. Admittedly, in a few references the verb means 'to prune' or 'cut off' but the word was not used of putting persons to death; it was used only of punishing people. Punishment, suffering and anguish, therefore, are denoted by the noun and verbal forms of *kolasis*.

c) *olethros*

Another Greek word sometimes misused by annihilationists is *olethros*. The apostle Paul uses the word in 2 Thessalonians 1:9 where it is translated as 'destruction': 'who shall be punished with everlasting destruction from the presence of the Lord . . .' William Hendriksen comments pertinently on Paul's use of the word in this verse: 'The very fact that this "destruction" is "everlasting" shows that it does not amount to "annihilation" or "going out of existence".'[9] On the contrary, it indicates an existence away from the presence of the Lord and from the glory of His power. Banishment away from the presence of the Lord is expulsion, not extinction.

The same word, *olethros*, is used in three other places in the New Testament, namely, 1 Thessalonians 5:3; 1 Timothy 6:9 and 1 Corinthians 5:5. Using the analogy of a woman with birth pangs, the first reference emphasizes the suddenness of the 'destruction' which will come upon

9. Hendriksen, *1 & 2 Thessalonians*, p.160.

unbelievers when Christ returns in glory. In 1 Timothy 6:9 'destruction' is linked with 'perdition' as awaiting those who are ruthlessly ambitious to become rich. The 1 Corinthians 5:5 reference is conclusive in showing that *olethros* cannot mean annihilation. Here the context is the apostle's direction to the Corinthian Christians to discipline the brother who had committed incest. They are told 'to deliver such an one unto Satan for the destruction of the flesh . . .' Quite clearly the word 'destruction' cannot mean annihilation for the man was to be restored later to church fellowship in 2 Corinthians 2:6-11. Furthermore, delivering the person 'to Satan' involved the church in withdrawing fellowship publicly from this brother, but the purpose was his own spiritual welfare and the triumphing of the spirit over the flesh in his life. Such 'destruction' of the flesh certainly involved anguish, chastening and repentance but not extinction.[10]

d) *she'ol*

As we saw in an earlier chapter, the Hebrew word *she'ol* occurs frequently in the Old Testament and, depending on the context, refers either to the grave or the state of death which all humans enter or to hell. It is this latter meaning of *she'ol* that many conditionalists as well as liberal scholars reject.

In Deuteronomy 32:22, for example, there is a reference to the lowest depths and the word *she'ol* draws attention here to the universality and severity of the divine wrath which burns against the wicked. Psalm 9:17 also uses *she'ol* in the sense of hell and this is supported by general references to the 'wicked' and 'all the nations'. Proverbs 15:11 uses both *she'ol* and *abaddon* ('destruction') in the Hebrew; the latter is a synonym for *she'ol* which emphasizes

10. An excellent example of the way in which classical Greek writers used *olethros* to refer to great and endless suffering is provided by R. C. Foster in *The Final Week* (Baker, 1962), p.118.

the condition rather than the place. Derek Kidner observes that there are nearly thirty references to 'death' and 'die' in Proverbs; there are also nine references to *she'ol*, two to *abaddon* and the pit, then *rephaim* (shades) is used three times. 'Among all these references', writes Kidner, 'there are few which limit their meaning beyond question to literal death.'[11]

Desmond Alexander draws attention to the importance of the Hebrew term for death, *māwet*, which has several connotations in the Old Testament.[12] In addition to the biological (Gen. 21:16), mythological (death as a power, agent or principle, Job 18:13; Jer. 9:21) and symbolical (Deut. 30:15; Psalm 13:3-4), Alexander refers to a fourth meaning as a place of existence after biological cessation (Job 38:17; Isa. 28:15).

Alexander questions the generally accepted view that all the dead, both the righteous and the wicked, go to *she'ol* but to different compartments there. This compartmentalized view of *she'ol* is not supported in the Old Testament and Alexander traces it back to the apocryphal book of 1 Enoch 22:1-14. At this point, Alexander is supported by A. Heidel who acknowledges various shades of meaning for *she'ol* yet concludes:

> as regards *she'ol* – we have evidence that it, in signification of the subterranean realm of the spirits, applies to the habitation of the souls of the wicked only.[13]

A clear distinction, therefore, is made between the destiny of the righteous and the wicked after death. Alexander strengthens Heidel's claim with two important observations. Firstly, apart from a few indecisive references (e.g. Eccl. 9:10; S. of S. 8:6), *she'ol* always conveys negative overtones (e.g. 2 Sam. 22:6; Psalm 16:10; 30:3; 86:13) and is the antithesis of heaven (e.g. Job 11:8; Ps. 139:8; Amos

11. Derek Kidner, *Proverbs*, Tyndale Commentary (IVP, 1971), p.65.
12. See *Themelios*, vol.2:2, January 1986.
13. ibid., p.43.

9:2)'.[14] Secondly, in a significant number of verses, *she'ol* is associated undeniably with evil-doers (e.g. Num. 16:30,33; 1 Kings 2:6,9; Job 24:19; Ps. 9:17; 31:17; 49:14; Prov. 5:5; 7:27; 9:18; Isa. 5:14; 14:9,11,15; Ezek. 31:15-17; 32:21,27). Here then is part of the evidence which points to the fact that, at times, *she'ol* refers to the 'ultimate abode of the wicked alone'.

We have widened the discussion somewhat in this section in order to show the rightness of the orthodox teaching concerning eternal punishment and thus expose the weaknesses in the conditionalists' argument from the language of Scripture. Now we return to Stott's arguments, particularly his next argument concerning the imagery of Scripture.

Imagery

Stott's second main argument concerns the imagery used in Scripture to characterize hell, especially that of fire. The main function of fire, he claims, is to destroy and he brings several objections against the doctrine of everlasting punishment in hell.[15]

a) Firstly, John Stott refers to Mark 9:48: 'where their worm dieth not, and the fire is not quenched'. His conclusion is that Jesus does not mention everlasting pain here in quoting Isaiah 66:24. The context of Isaiah 66 is, however, ideal for the use which our Lord makes of verse 24 in Mark 9:44,46 and 48. Two truths are emphasized there. One is the glorious blessing and deliverance of God's people; the other is the judgment and punishment of unbelievers in which the valley of Hinnom/Gehenna is used figuratively. It is true that the physical death of unbelievers is mentioned in the Isaiah text but there is more. Beyond physical death, unbelievers will still suffer and the

14. ibid., p.44.
15. Edwards and Stott, *Essentials*, pp.316-18.

language of 'worms' and 'fire' points to this. Do the 'worms' point to guilty, tormented consciences? Notice, too, how the Greek word, *gehenna* ('hell'), is used three times by the Lord in verses 43, 45 and 47; the danger of being 'cast into hell fire' is an awful reality for people. 'Fire' in the context of hell refers to God's wrath upon sin: 'our God is a consuming fire' (Hebrews 12:29). Observe how our Lord stresses five times in Mark 9 that 'the fire . . . never shall be quenched', thus underlining the permanence both of divine wrath and the conscious punishment of unbelievers.

b) Next, John Stott refers to Matthew 25:46: 'and these shall go away into everlasting punishment'.

It is worth quoting Stott's comments on this verse in full:

> Does that not indicate that in hell people endure eternal conscious punishment? No, that is to read into the text what is not necessarily there. What Jesus said is that both the life and the punishment would be eternal, but he did not in that passage define the nature of either. Because he elsewhere spoke of eternal life as a conscious enjoyment of God (John 17:3), it does not follow that eternal punishment must be a conscious experience of pain at the hand of God. On the contrary, although declaring both to be eternal, is contrasting the two destinies: the more unlike they are, the better.[16]

Concerning the nature of hell in verse 46, our Lord tells us succinctly that it involves 'punishment' and is 'eternal'. Stott's argument, however, is a weak one. For example, he gives no reason why eternal punishment should not be 'a conscious experience of pain at the hand of God'. True, the Lord is contrasting two destinies but what could be more dissimilar than the conscious enjoyment of God by believers in heaven and, on the other hand, the conscious suffering of unbelievers in hell? Such contrasting experiences are literally worlds apart.

16. ibid., p.317.

139

c) Stott proceeds to argue his case from Luke 16:23-28. He proceeds more cautiously at this point and great caution is needed in interpreting this passage. One important reason for caution is that the Lord is teaching by way of analogy and some of the details cannot be pressed. But this is not a parable and our Lord does not Himself introduce it as a parable. What is more, this passage is unlike the parables of the Lord Jesus. In parables, He *never* named individuals and confined the parables to people, incidents and details in *this* life, not in the after-life. These verses in Luke 16 may well be an illustration of our Lord speaking of the 'heavenly' and other-worldly things referred to in John 3:12. Paterson Smyth is justified in affirming of Luke 16:23ff.: 'This is a direct statement about the invisible things themselves. Jesus is telling what happens after death.'[17]

Three basic principles emerge in this statement by the Lord: the conscious continuing existence of unbelievers and believers after death, the suffering of unbelievers in hell and, finally, their irreversible state. Stott comes much nearer here to the orthodox position but wrongly assumes that because the word 'hades' is used for 'hell' in verse 23 then this must refer only to the interim period between death and final judgment when eventually the unbelievers will be annihilated. The whole tenor and language of Luke 16:23ff. is against Stott's conclusion. Hades is used here to describe the abode and punishment of the ungodly in the intermediate state before the general resurrection of the body and Stott acknowledges the point. Gehenna is used, however, to describe this same continuous punishment after the final judgment when both body *and* soul will be punished in hell.

We conclude, therefore, that the imagery used in Scripture to characterize hell does not support the theory of annihilation.

17. J. Paterson Smyth, *The Gospel of the Hereafter*, p.61.

3. Theological arguments

There are two theological arguments Stott uses in favour of the concept of annihilation.

The first argument concerns **justice** and **sin**.

Justice, he believes, is more consistent with annihilation than with everlasting punishment. His main supporting point is the 'serious disproportion between sins consciously committed in time and torment consciously experienced throughout eternity'.[18] This same argument is used but with greater vigour by Arthur Custance.

Custance refers to the legal principle that the magnitude of an offence is related to the dignity of the one against whom the offence is committed. On this principle, varying degrees of seriousness and anger are expressed depending on whether one has offended against an animal or a human, between a relatively poor person or a representative person like a mayor, a Member of Parliament or a member of the royal family. Custance writes:

> When a man offends against God the offence is qualitatively maximized to infinity, for the honour of God is infinite. Such an offence is an offence against the Creator Himself and against all his creatures as well, for his honour is in a measure wrapped up in them all. Thus no greater offence is conceivable.[19]

Custance then asks whether the magnitude of the offence is to be measured in terms of quantity or quality and punished accordingly eternally in hell (quantity) or annihilated (quality). He concludes that 'the demand for endless punishment for a temporal offence cannot be justified merely on the grounds that the offence has been against an infinite Majesty'.[20]

18. Edwards and Stott, *Essentials*, p.318
19. Custance, *The Sovereignty of Grace*, p.318.
20. ibid., p.319.

Reply

By way of reply, a number of points need to be made. To begin with, the phrase 'temporal offence' is unhelpful and misleading. For one thing it tends to minimize the seriousness of sin and both Stott and Custance are aware of the danger. Furthermore, expressed in the singular form, the phrase 'temporal offence' hides the fact that sinners are born in sin and also sin against God continually throughout their lives. While 'temporal' draws attention to the fact that people sin in this temporal life yet the law they break is divine and has eternal consequences. Added to this is the fact that the term 'temporal' is too restrictive because sinners continue to sin even in hell. While they submit unwillingly to God's reign there and express remorse because of their fate, yet they are never born again of the Spirit nor converted in hell. In other words, whatever divine restraints and punishments are inflicted upon them they remain sinful and continue to sin against God. John Stott acknowledges that his own argument here is weakened if one insists on 'the impenitence of the lost . . . through eternity'.[21] Again, Custance's criticism of the orthodox position that the infinite majesty of God is related to the seriousness of human sin and its necessary eternal punishment in hell is not convincing.

First of all, categories of sin are distinguished in the Bible, particularly sins of ignorance and presumption (Num. 15:22-36; Luke 23:34; 1 Tim. 1:13; etc.) but, in addition, sinning against certain persons was regarded as being more serious. An obvious example is Miriam's criticism of the Lord's servant, Moses (Num. 12:1-16) or David's refusal to kill Saul: 'the Lord forbid that I should do this thing to my master, the Lord's anointed, to stretch forth my hand against him, seeing he is the anointed of the Lord' (1 Sam. 24:6). The principle is expressed further in

21. Edwards and Stott, *Essentials,* p.319.

relation to the Lord Jesus Christ. It was 'the Lord of glory' (1 Cor. 2:8), the One who 'was rich' (2 Cor. 8:9) and 'in the form of God' (Phil. 2:6) who was crucified. This fact not only heightens the wickedness of His crucifiers but it also means that the Saviour's sacrifice for our sins has infinite value because of His divine Person. Against this scriptural background, therefore, one can see more clearly that sin against the infinite majesty of God incurs everlasting punishment.

The second argument concerns **the final victory of God over evil**.

'The eternal existence of the impenitent in hell', writes Stott, 'would be hard to reconcile with the promise of God's final victory over evil . . .'[22] Similarly, Custance claims that if unbelievers are punished for ever in hell then 'the universe will never be free of the presence of evil and the Lord's victory will never be truly complete'.[23]

This objection is flawed in several ways. To begin with, it imposes an unbiblical interpretation on the promise of God's final victory over evil by assuming that it necessarily entails the elimination of all sinners and sin. 2 Peter 3:13 teaches there will be 'new heavens and a new earth wherein dwelleth righteousness' only, but this does not contradict the existence of hell nor the conscious punishment of sinners there. God's victory will be complete even in hell. Another important consideration concerns God's own glorification in the just punishment of sinners in hell as well as in the glorification of His church. This truth is taught throughout the Bible and is clearly expressed, for example, in Romans 9:21-23. At the end, Christ's lordship will be acknowledged universally, though in different ways and for different reasons; at such a time, God will be glorified in the display of His wrath as well as of His mercy.

22. ibid., p.319.
23. Custance, *The Sovereignty of Grace*, p.354.

Conclusion

By way of conclusion, we refer to three writers who have wrestled with the biblical data on the subject of hell.

Paul Helm writes:

> Scripture teaches that the impenitent wicked will suffer (Luke 16:23). But it is impossible to suffer if one does not exist. And the suffering indicated is everlasting, corresponding to the everlasting life enjoyed by the redeemed, as Scripture explicitly teaches (Matt. 25:46). In the face of both the weakness of the arguments for annihilationism, and the strength of the arguments against, one is forced to reject it.[24]

The American theologian, Kenneth S. Kantzer, writes similarly:

> Those who acknowledge Jesus Christ as Lord cannot escape the clear, unambiguous language with which He warns of the awful truth of eternal punishment. No universalism, no probation in the hereafter satisfies His Word. The awful stark destiny of man is this: The soul that rebels against God and . . . remains unrepentant throughout this life will separate himself from the kingdom of God.[25]

The last quotation is from J.I. Packer:

> What troubles me most . . . is the assumption of superior sensitivity by the Conditionalists. Their assumption appears in the adjectives (awful, dreadful . . . intolerable, etc.) that they apply to the concept of eternal punishment, as if to suggest that holders of the historic view have never thought about the meaning of what they have been saying. John Stott records his belief 'that the ultimate annihilation of the wicked should be accepted as a legitimate, biblically founded alternative to their eternal conscious torment.' Respectfully, I disagree, for the biblical arguments are to my mind flimsy special pleading and the feelings that make people want conditionalism to be true seem to me to

24. Helm, *The Last Things*, p.119.
25. *Christianity Today*, vol.35:5, 20 March 1987, p.45.

reflect, not superior spiritual sensitivity, but secular sentimentalism which assumes that in heaven our feelings about others will be as at present, and our joy in the manifesting of God's justice will be no greater than it is now. It is certainly agonizing now to live with the thought of people going to an eternal hell, but it is not right to reduce the agony by evading the facts; and in heaven . . . the agony will be a thing of the past.[26]

6. Kantzer and Henry (eds.), *Evangelical Affirmations*, pp.125-6.

11
Hell

Its challenge

We must now apply the doctrine of hell in more detail to evangelistic preaching, and then to the need of compassion and zeal in the church for reaching hell-bound sinners with the gospel of Jesus Christ. First of all, however, a note of warning must be sounded concerning the implications of rejecting or modifying the orthodox, biblical doctrine of hell.

A word of caution

To those tempted to abandon the traditional view, John W. Wenham has provided a much needed caution. He warns, for example, of the danger of twisting clear statements of Scripture, and allowing our thinking to be dominated by contemporary liberal thought rather than by the Word of God. Wenham also observes that the revival of conditionalism earlier this century was pioneered largely by Socinians and Arians, who at the same time rejected such fundamental doctrines as the deity of Christ. 'Be wary', he adds, 'of such bedfellows.'[1] That Jehovah's Witnesses, Christadelphians and Seventh Day Adventists all teach conditionalism rather than eternal punishment is significant, and this fact must be regarded as a warning to Christians not to compromise in the smallest detail with biblical truth.

I cannot agree with Wenham's conclusion that Seventh Day Adventists 'stand essentially in the broad stream of traditional evangelicalism, having eccentricities which may

1. Wenham, *The Goodness of God*, p.38.

be regarded as more or less peripheral'.[2] The contemporary crisis within Adventism only confirms the fact that the group has neither accepted nor taught consistently such basic truths as justification by faith, the sufficiency of Christ's atoning sacrifice, or the supreme authority of the Bible in contrast to the writings of its leader Mrs Ellen White, which have hitherto been regarded as sacrosanct. These differences are by no means 'peripheral'. In a different category, admittedly, are Jehovah's Witnesses and Christadelphians; as well as the doctrine of hell, these two heretical sects reject the Trinity, the deity of Christ, the personality and deity of the Holy Spirit, justification by faith, the sufficiency of Christ's atoning death, total depravity and the necessity of regeneration.

It is invariably true that the rejection of the orthodox doctrine of hell involves also the rejection of other foundational truths. A writer in the *Christian Remembrancer* for April 1863 confirms this fact and avows that 'we have not been able to discover a single impugner of the dogma of eternal punishment who is consistent in his denial, and at the same time orthodox'. Seventeen years later, E.M. Goulbourn made the same point, but in more detail:

> It is a dangerous thing to meddle with the theology of the Bible; because all its doctrines, though many of them soar far beyond us into the region of mystery, are yet so wonderfully coherent that to touch one is to imperil the rest. Scriptural theology resembles an arch, so constructed that all the great stones shall be keystones. Displace any of these stones, and you will find that the whole fabric falls to pieces under your hands. Dislodge the doctrine of eternal punishment from the system of scriptural theology, and you will find, if you employ against it similar objections, that the Atonement itself begins to give way; for if you are determined to reject the idea of a finite sin having an infinite penalty, you will find it at least equally hard, or even more hard,

2. ibid., p.38.

to understand how a finite sin can demand an infinitely precious Sacrifice. But the Atonement is not the only fundamental doctrine which you shake by dislodging that of eternal punishment.[3]

Recent history and trends in our country confirm Goulbourn's statement. Earlier this century many churches rejected the doctrine of eternal punishment, and not long afterwards these same churches began to question and then reject other basic doctrines, with the result that most church denominations are now apostate. It is an alarming fact that some evangelicals today dislike the biblical doctrine of hell; but their theological position in other respects is equally disturbing, for they also deny doctrines like inerrancy, total depravity, etc. It is essential, then, for believers to embrace the orthodox doctrine of hell, not only because it is scriptural, but for the added reason that this doctrine is interrelated with other key doctrines (such as the wrath of God, the Trinity, the atonement, justification by faith, the doctrine of Scripture) and is dependent upon them.

Evangelistic preaching

This doctrine also has a bearing upon the content and urgency of evangelistic preaching. Although a preacher may not *deny* the orthodox doctrine of hell, yet he still needs to ask himself whether he preaches it with the clarity, frequency and urgency that God demands. 'The hearers are led to deny the truth which the preacher leaves out of his sermon,' was the perceptive observation of John Elias, to which he added, 'Omitting truth intentionally in a sermon leads to the denial of it.'[4] In the same context Elias speaks of the deficiencies of many preachers. He laments the fact, for example, that 'it is not plainly declared that all

3. E.M. Goulbourn, *Everlasting Punishment* (London: Rivingtons, 1880), p.26.
4. Edward Morgan, *John Elias, Life and Letters*, p.354.

the human race are by nature "the children of wrath", and that the "sentence of condemnation" is passed on every one; that none can save himself; that no one deserves to be rescued, and that none will come to Christ to have life.'[5] The preacher needs to examine his preaching in the light of this lament, for he may believe the right things about hell, and yet fail to preach it as an integral part of the gospel message. The warning of Professor John Murray at this point is pertinent:

> A conspicuous defect . . . is the absence of warning and of condemnation in evangelistic effort. The naturalistic temper of our age, united with its callousness, makes the doctrine of hell peculiarly uncongenial. It is more often the subject of crude jest than it is of solemn warning or foreboding. The supposed politeness of modern etiquette has too often succeeded in creating the sentiment that any serious reference to hell and damnation is not accordant with the canons of good taste. These evils have in many cases ensnared even the orthodox.

> But hell is an unspeakable reality and, if evangelism is to march on its way, it must by God's grace produce that sense of condemnation complexioned by the apprehension of perdition as the due reward of sin. For it is in the anguish of such a sense of condemnation, in the anguish of a conscience that stings with the apprehension of the wrath and curse of God, that the gospel of God's free grace becomes as cold water to a thirsty soul and as good news from a far country.[6]

We must then be thoroughly biblical and orthodox in doctrine and, at the same time, faithful in the proclamation of this divinely given message.

Our attention can now be turned to practical matters, such as warning, simplicity and directness in the preaching of hell, as well as the need of compassion for the lost.

5. ibid., p.354.
6. *Collected Writings of John Murray* (Banner of Truth, 1976), vol.1, p.130.

Warning

The note of warning must be sounded loud and clear in our preaching. Although we are accused of using the doctrines of wrath and hell in order to frighten people into the kingdom of God, our real purpose is to warn sinners of their danger and of their urgent need to trust in Christ for salvation. Furthermore, this is something which God commands us to do. It was God Himself who warned Adam and Eve of the punishment their sin would receive; He also sent Jonah to warn Nineveh of impending judgment; and Jesus Christ during His earthly ministry frequently warned people of the consequences of unbelief and sin (see, for example, Matthew 7:13-14; Luke 13:1-5, and John 3:15-18). Preachers, however, sometimes feel unsure as to the way in which they should issue this warning to sinners, and they are in need of both encouragement and guidance.

Simplicity and directness

Jonathan Edwards's 'strategy' in preaching hell is helpful at this point. There is, he argues, a spiritual reality about hell that can affect most unconverted people. The motivating principle of humans is self-interest, and matters concerning their welfare or doom are of the utmost importance to them. Being in their natural state, men and women cannot see God's excellency, but they can most certainly hear His thunders. So Edwards argues that good, practical use should be made of the doctrine of hell in evangelistic preaching.[7] He himself shows us how it should be done. Preaching on Ezekiel 22:14 with the express purpose of revealing the unavoidable and intolerable punishment of the wicked in hell, Edwards asks his hearers to imagine themselves being thrown into a fiery oven or a great furnace for a quarter of an hour:

7. Gerstner, *Jonathan Edwards on Heaven and Hell*, p.181.

What horror would you feel! . . . And after you had endured it for one minute, how overbearing would it be to you to think that you had to endure the other four-teen!

But what would be the effect on your soul, if you knew you must lie there enduring that torment to the full for twenty-four hours ... a whole year ... a thou-sand years! – O then, how would your hearts sink if you knew that you must bear it for ever and ever! that there would be no end! that after millions of millions of ages, your torment would be no nearer to an end, and that you never, never should be delivered!

But your torment in hell will be immensely greater than this illustration represents ...

You who now hear of hell and the wrath of the great God, and sit here so easy and quiet, and go away so careless; by and by will shake and tremble, and cry out, and shriek, and gnash your teeth, and will be thor-oughly convinced of the vast weight and importance of these things which you now despise.[8]

Clearly part of Edwards's strategy in preaching hell was the telling use of illustrations, to warn and enforce the doctrine with a sustained application at a level and in a language the people understood. In addition, such plain and direct talking was accompanied by deep concern, expressed particularly in pleading with his hearers.

Another preacher gifted in this respect was Charles Haddon Spurgeon. In his sermon on Matthew 8:11-12, for example, describing those who will be cast out when they arrive at heaven's gates, he pictures Justice saying, 'There he comes! there he comes! he spurned a father's prayers, and mocked a mother's tears.' He then goes on to under-line the eternity of hell, where sinners have no hope:

They have not even the hope of dying – the hope of being annihilated. They are for ever – for ever – for ever – lost! On every chain in hell, there is written 'for ever'.

8. *The Works of Jonathan Edwards*, vol.2, pp.81-3.

In the fires, there blaze out the words 'for ever'. Up
above their heads, they read, 'for ever' . . . Oh! if I could
tell you tonight that hell would one day be burned out,
and that those who were lost might be saved, there
would be a jubilee in hell at the very thought of it. But it
cannot be – it is **'for ever'** they are 'cast into outer
darkness'.[9]

In this sermon Spurgeon remonstrates with the old men
in his congregation, beseeching them to consider their
danger: 'Let me warn you, grey-headed men; your evening
is coming. O poor tottering grey-head, wilt thou take the
last step into the pit? Let a young child step before thee
and beg thee to consider . . .' Here is another aspect of the
'strategy' in preaching hell, namely, the importance of
exhorting and warning each age-group and class of people
in the congregation in a searching application of the Word.

Compassion for the lost

Some of the Welsh preachers in the eighteenth and nineteenth centuries were masters of the art of applying the
gospel to their hearers. One of them, the Rev. Jenkin
Jones, although an Arminian, was a popular and effective
preacher of the gospel. Ordained in 1726 to the Welsh
Congregational ministry in West Wales, he had a tremen-
dous passion and zeal for the lost, and this was naturally
expressed in his preaching and writing. Picturing the separation of believers and unbelievers at the second coming of
the Lord, he describes the reaction of the unbelievers when
they see the elect taken up into the air to be with Christ:
'O! take us up with you. What are you doing leaving us
behind?' At this point the preacher hears their cry of
anguish and replies:

What can I do for you? I must tell you that I told you
these things before, but you did not consider them. I

9. C.H. Spurgeon, *New Park Street Pulpit* (Banner of Truth, 1963), vol. 1
(1855), pp.307ff.

called you to repentance and preached Christ to you and showed to you the way of salvation, but you did not accept Him . . . O, what can I do with you now? . . . Now it is too late . . . What can I do? You know how I endangered my life because of you to preach to you . . . but now the treasury of the gospel is sealed up and the day of grace has passed . . .[10]

Repeatedly the preacher expresses his anguish and perplexity as he sees these unbelievers being separated from the elect and later sent into hell. In this man's ministry there was much more than directness, simplicity and application; his heart was burning with compassion for the lost, in the realization of their awful danger outside of Christ.

Is it not here that many preachers fail? Applying the gospel and pleading with sinners is more than a technique and more than oratory; it is essentially the language of a heart stirred and deeply affected by the gospel. Paradoxically, orthodoxy is both essential and inadequate, for the truth must also be *felt* by the preacher before he will be able to warn and exhort sinners effectively. In other words, if the gospel is to be preached as God intends it, the essential qualities required are compassion coupled with a deep sense of urgency. Here and now God intends that His people love and care for unbelievers. There can be no excuse for indifference or cold professionalism among preachers. Their hearts must throb with the love of God. Dare one speak of the Lord's infinite love and the Saviour's glorious sacrifice with lips and hearts unmoved towards the lost? Compassion is required of us *now*, before it is too late. In heaven we will not need compassion for the lost; there, we shall exult in God and His glory, shown not only in our salvation but also in the just damnation of those in hell. Compassion for the lost, therefore, is confined to this

10. Thomas Vincent, *Christ's Certain and Sudden Appearance to Judgment* (1667) – quoted from the Welsh translation by Jenkin Jones, *Dydd y Farn Fawr* (1727), pp.61-101.

world, where the doors of heaven are still open to repenting sinners.

During his first furlough in England, Hudson Taylor addressed a large missionary conference in Scotland. He began his talk by relating the story of a Chinese man who fell into a dangerous river in China and was allowed to drown by a number of indifferent onlookers. The conference members were, of course, disgusted to hear of this callous indifference on the part of the bystanders. Hudson Taylor lost no time in applying his illustration. 'You are very upset by their refusal to rescue a drowning man from physical death,' he said, 'but what of your indifference to the spiritual death and hopelessness of thousands and thousands who die each year in China without ever hearing of the Lord Jesus?'

Hell is an awful reality, and without Christ it is to hell that men and women will go, whether they live in China or Wales or any other part of the world. It is the duty of all believers, and especially preachers, to love and warn and rescue people from hell. I know it is only God who saves, but let us not hide behind the sovereignty of God. The sovereign God who elects sinners has also sovereignly appointed prayer, preaching, witnessing, etc., as the means by which He will gather in His elect, and we must therefore be diligent and zealous in the use of these means.

It is also true that compassion belongs to the very nature of God, and only God can give it to His people. However hard we may try, it is impossible for us to work up genuine compassion for unbelievers. But the challenge remains. Are we imploring God for more and more of His compassion? Do we repent of our indifference? Are our hearts and lives right before Him?

Each year, at least 30 million people throughout the world die. Each time the second finger of my watch moves, a person dies and goes to either heaven or hell. Do we cry to God for the conversion of these people, and are we doing our utmost to reach them with the gospel? One thing is clear. The days and months and years are speeding by for all of us. Soon our time on earth will end and 'every man's work shall be made manifest'. Our responsiblities are onerous indeed. It is time for us to reappraise our priorities, and to give ourselves wholeheartedly to the Lord and His gospel for the salvation of the lost before the end comes.

General Index

Adam, 65-6, 70, 78, 116, 125, 150
Alexander, D. & Heidel, A., 137-8
America/American, 10, 15, 17-18, 21-2, 24, 27, 40, 45, 144
Anabaptist, 23, 40
Anaxagoras, 56
Anderson, N., 12, 15, 47-8
Angel/s, 58, 79, 84-6, 88, 103, 112, 120
  fallen angels, 40, 68, 88, 98, 109, 117
Anger, of God, 70, 73, 77, 120 (*see also* Wrath)
Anglican, 10, 13-14, 26, 28, 122
Angus, Dr, 30
Annihilation, 9-22, 23, 30, 74, 98, 100, 108, 111, 118-20, 121, 126, 132-45, 151 (*see also* Extinction)
Anonymous Christians, 47-8
Apocrypha, 137
Ariarajah, W., 51
Arndt & Gingrich, 130
Atkinson, B., 11-12
Atonement, 25, 27, 126, 147-8
Augustine, 40, 118
Authority, 63, 67-8, 78, 85, 87, 104, 108, 147
Axial period, 51

Baha'i, 44
Baille, D.M., 34
Bampton Lectures, 26
Baptists, 28-30, 33
Barclay, William, 34, 45-6
Barth, K., 34, 41, 45-6, 57, 121
Bateson, B., 11-13
Bauckham, R.J., 39, 49
Baxter, Richard, 28
Bengel, 89
Benton, John 20
Berkhof, H., 34
Berkhof, L., 100-1, 114, 127, 128-9

Bernard, J.H., 57
Biblical teaching, 55-69, 70-82, 83-97, 98-107, 108-20, 121-31, 134-44, 150-1
Birks, T.R., 27-8
Blaiklock, E.M., 62
Bolton, Samuel, 78
Boston, Thomas, 114, 120
Bray, Gerald, 53
Britain/British, 43-4, 49-50, 122 (*see also* England/English)
British & Foreign Schools Society, 29
British Council of Churches (BCC), 44
Brown, Colin, 57
Bruce, F.F., 60
Brunner, Emil, 12
Buddhism/Buddhist, 44, 49-52
Buiss, H., 15-16
Bunyan, John, 104

Calvin/ism, 15, 29
Carson, Don, 21
Cassell & Co. (Publishers), 31-3
Cavallin, H.C.C., 126
Chalcedon, 48, 50, 53
Christ, 52-4, 55-60, 63-9, 73-4, 85-92, 100-6, 108-18, 124-5, 136, 143, 147, 150
  Cosmic Christ, 63-4
Christadelphians, 98, 146-7
Christian World, 30
Christianity, 42-53, 126
Christians, anonymous, 42, 47-8
Christology, 45-6, 50, 52-3, 60
Chrysostom, 89
Church, 109-10
  Church of England – *see* Anglican
Clark, R.E.D., 11, 13
Clark, Samuel, 23
Clayton, George, 29

Index to Scripture References

Index to Hebrew Words

Index to Greek Words

Books by J. Douglas MacMillan
published by the Evangelical Press of Wales

THE LORD OUR SHEPHERD

The author's first-hand experience as a shepherd makes this study of Psalm 23 a truly inspiring book.

'spiritually and psychologically refreshing . . . unique . . .'
(*Peace and Truth*)

'warm, devotional, doctrinal preaching at its best'
(*Grace Magazine*)

'a banquet to the hungry and thirsty soul'   (*Banner of Truth*)

'a very inspiring little book'   (*English Churchman*)

WRESTLING WITH GOD

Sub-titled 'Lessons from the Life of Jacob', this book gives deep spiritual insights into the experiences of Jacob at Bethel and Peniel.

'wonderfully fresh and vital . . . searching and challenging . . .
it would not be possible to recommend this book too highly'
(*Evangelical Presbyterian*)

'a delightful book . . . warmly commended' (*Gospel Magazine*)

'a valuable book'   (*Banner of Truth*)

JESUS – POWER WITHOUT MEASURE

Sub-titled 'The Work of the Spirit in the Life of our Lord', this absorbing and illuminating book works chronologically through the life of Christ, studying the role of the Spirit in relation to his life and ministry. A remarkable book, charting relatively unexplored waters.

'a unique contribution to our understanding of the role of the Holy Spirit'   (*Christian Arena*)

'it takes us into the deep mysteries of the revealed Word . . .
[and] is to be much commended'   (*Gospel Magazine*)

'a helpful and inspiring book'   (*Evangelical Times*)

'a profound book with valuable insights'   (*Evangelicals Now*)

CHRISTIAN HYMNS

Paul E. G. Cook and
Graham Harrison (editors)

Over 100,000 copies of *Christian Hymns* have been sold since it was first published in 1977. The warm reception given to it by both churches and the Christian press confirm the view of many that it is one of the finest hymn-books available today.

- Comprehensive selection of 900 hymns.
- Suitable for public worship and informal church gatherings.
- Includes 80 metrical psalms and paraphrases.
- Useful children's section.
- Beautifully printed and strongly bound.

Available in
Standard, de-luxe and large-type words editions
and a slim-line music edition

CHRISTIAN HYMN-WRITERS

Elsie Houghton

The stories behind some of the great hymns are often as inspiring as the hymns themselves. This fascinating book takes us 'behind the scenes' and enables us to appreciate much more those words with which we are so familiar. In brief but telling biographies, the author covers a wide range of hymn-writers from the early centuries of the Christian church down to the twentieth century. This popular work comes complete with a valuable index, and has now been reprinted with a bright new cover.

Further titles from the Evangelical Press of Wales

In the Shadow of Aran by Mari Jones. Stories from farm life in the Welsh mountains which present spiritual truths vividly.

They Beheld His Glory by Peter Trumper. A thrilling look at the birth of the Saviour through the eyes of some of those intimately involved.

God Cares by Brian Edwards. A practical exposition of Psalm 106.

The Holiness of God and of His People by Hugh D. Morgan. A warm, practical application of the Bible's teaching on an all-important subject.

One Bible, One Message? by Bryan A. Williams. This book looks at a number of central truths and clearly demonstrates the complete agreement of the Old and New Testaments on these matters.

To Bala for a Bible by Elisabeth Williams. The true story of Mary Jones and the beginnings of the Bible Society.

The Welsh Revival of 1904 by Eifion Evans. A thorough but readable study of the 1904 Revival. Foreword by D.M. Lloyd-Jones.

Revival Comes to Wales by Eifion Evans. A gripping account of the mighty working of God the Holy Spirit in Wales during the 1859 Revival.

Two Welsh Revivalists by Eifion Evans. The fascinating stories of Humphrey Jones and Dafydd Morgan, the two prominent leaders during the 1859 Revival in Wales.

Howell Harris and the Dawn of Revival by Richard Bennett. A study of the early spiritual life of Howell Harris and the beginnings of the Great Awakening of the eighteenth century in Wales.

'Excuse Me, Mr Davies—Hallelujah!' by Geraint D. Fielder; foreword by Lady Catherwood. The absorbing story of evangelical student witness in Wales in the twentieth century, a story which includes periods of quite remarkable spiritual blessing.

Christian Family Matters edited by Ian Shaw, foreword by Sir Frederick Catherwood. Clear biblical guidelines by experienced contributors on such matters as marriage, parenthood, divorce and adoption.

Social Issues and the Local Church edited by Ian Shaw. Subjects covered include the state, work, education, mission, social welfare and the role of women in the local church.

The Christian Heritage of Welsh Education by R.M. Jones & Gwyn Davies. A bird's-eye view of Christian education in Wales down the centuries.

Gospel and Church by Hywel R. Jones. An evangelical evaluation of ecumenical documents on church unity.

The Evangelical Magazine of Wales. A bimonthly magazine with a wide range of articles on all aspects of Christian faith and life.